An
Encyclopedia
of Love

An Encyclopedia of Love

(in one volume)

M. Scheil
General Editor

Picador USA
New York

Picador® is a U.S. registered trademark and is used by St. Martin's Press under license from Pan Books Limited.

For information on Picador USA Reading Group Guides, as well as ordering, please contact the Trade Marketing department at St. Martin's Press.
Phone: 1-800-221-7945 extension 763
Fax: 212-677-7456
E-mail: trademarketing@stmartins.com

Design by James Sinclair

Library of Congress Cataloging-in-Publication Data

Scheil, M.
    An encyclopedia of love : (in one volume) / M. Scheil, general editor.
      p. cm.
    Includes index.
    ISBN 0-312-19871-X (hc)
    ISBN 0-312-25283-8 (pbk)
    1. Love stories. I. Title.
PS3569.C4854E53 1999
818'.5407 dc 21   98-041753
                                    CIP

First Picador USA Paperback Edition: January 2000

10 9 8 7 6 5 4 3 2 1

CONTENTS

INTRODUCTION

An Encyclopedia of Love is a compilation of factual and semifactual paragraphs concerning a single, heterosexual relationship from its inception to its conclusion upon the death (some two years later) of one of the partners. While items are included that both pre- and postdate the two years in question, the *Encyclopedia* is neither intended nor arranged as a chronological narrative. There is, moreover, not the intention of other encyclopedias to be objective about the information presented. All articles are written by the surviving partner and rely solely on her memory and point of view. Discussion of persons incidental to the relationship (friends and relations) is, for the most part, omitted as are the names of the partners themselves. All entries are in the third person.

There are twenty-two subjects in the *Encyclopedia,* arranged alphabetically. Twelve of these are further subdivided (depending on complexity of subject), and each includes a general summary before moving on to individual entries (see Reader's Guide, p. xi).

The general schema of the *Encyclopedia* runs as follows:

$\mathcal{A}$ Abilities
Art
        (a) Concepts   (d) Materials
        (b) Elements   (e) Styles
        (c) Form   (f) Subjects
Attitudes

$\mathcal{B}$ Beliefs
Biography
        (a) Hers
        (b) His
        (c) Joint

In all, the *Encyclopedia* contains twenty-two summaries, approximately 450 entries, and a comprehensive alphabetical index. Overlapping subjects are cross-referenced wherever possible.

—M. Scheil

READER'S GUIDE

1. The *Encyclopedia* is divided by (a) alphabet letter; (b) subject matter (under a general heading); (c) summary; (d) subcategory or -categories; and (e) entries.

2. Summaries are intended either to outline information given in the entries or to provide information in their own right, giving an overview of the subject as well as facts and opinions not contained elsewhere under the heading.

3. With the exception of (a) recipes listed under Cookery; (b) phrases where the heading or subcategory makes plain the missing noun; or (c) where common usage dictates that the adjective precede the noun, proper or common nouns are used to determine the alphabetical position of entry listings with more than one word.

4. A list of illustrations is found below.

5. Cross-references appear at the ends of both summaries and entries.

6. The *Encyclopedia* is not intended to be read from first page to last. Rather, the reader is encouraged to dip into subjects at random, allowing them, cross-references, or even index listings to lead where they will (*see* Introduction, pp. vii–ix).

ILLUSTRATIONS

Art
Figure 1: Sketch for a projected "Aura" portrait (see Concepts: Imagination, p. 8).

Figure 2: Example of cross-hatching—"Weather Through Windows" (*see* Elements: Line, p. 11).

Figure 3: Example of a large pine structure (*see* Form: Sculpture, p. 13).

Figure 4: Example of a landscape from the group of island drawings (*see* Subject: Landscape, p. 19).

A ....

*A*bilities

Summary
Happily, the abilities of one partner fully complemented those of the other, for example, he could do anything with his hands whereas she was superior in all forms of communication and financial organisation. It was generally acknowledged by both that together they constituted a sort of prodigy insofar as domestic life was concerned. During their time together, each one attempted to instruct the other in the skills that the other didn't possess. That the results of such tuition were marginal can be attributed to limitations in worldview rather than intelligence or dexterity. Looking at the twelve skills listed (and without assigning greater importance to any one or group of them), she tended to assume she was the more fortunate as he boasted eight as compared to her competence in only four. He, on the other hand, was morbidly conscious of his shortcomings in those four and would have never entertained a notion of superiority based simply on numbers (*see* Biography/His: various; Character: Organisation; and Self-image/Contributing to: various).

Baking: Biscuits (American style), rock cakes, and scones were his specialties, though at both Christmases he also made mince pies (both individual size and 9″ diameter) for their guests. His struggle with the pastry was as much a fixture as the pies themselves in that he would insist on pure ingredients, but also on the flaky consistency that only adulterated products seemed to offer. Believing that sheer persistence could overcome the contradiction, he would attempt pie after pie with varying success, though even his densest pastry was usually edible. The same cannot be said, however, of the breads he tried during their time together. Regardless of recipe, he invariably produced doughs that either didn't rise at all or else violently overflowed whatever containers they had been set in. The finished product, if not technically uncuttable the day it was baked, became so the morning after. Under his patient instruction she began to make biscuits and scones, although she wouldn't attempt either without his presence in the kitchen, or farther away than two adjoining rooms (*see* Diet/Compulsive/Harmful: Cakes/Cookies; Diet/Regimens, various; and Passions/Holidays: Christmas).

Carpentry: *See* Passions/Art: Wood and Work/His: Carpentry, Joinery.

Communication, verbal: Of the pair, she was by far the more verbal and extroverted. He knew that when introducing her to his friends or acquaintances she would inevitably make a good impression, and that communications he found unpleasant or awkward—such as repeatedly cancelling dental appointments or demanding money he was owed—could be left to her with impunity. He also knew that at other times she was incapable of controlling her tongue. Three instances of this he found particularly irritating were (1) having his sentences finished for him; (2) not being allowed to speak at all; and (3) being forcibly included in conversations with third parties. When admonished, she duly acknowledged that such practices were inexcusable and that she would make every effort to desist from them in the future. That future did not arrive during his lifetime (*see* Biography/His: School; Character: various; and Love/Specifics: Talking).

Computer: Use of a personal computer illustrates an interesting crossover in both the skills and deficiencies of the couple. As she was a writer, he had always found it surprising she didn't own one while she herself had acknowledged its utility to the extent of becoming marginally literate in a software language. That notwithstanding, the whole concept of personal computers and all that went along with them remained an exotic idea for the pair. Buying the necessary hardware required jargon neither could easily master, and a mass of conflicting opinions from all sorts of veterans tended to further reduce their confidence. When the hardware was finally purchased and needed to be set up, his mechanical skills instinctively surfaced, and he managed it with hardly a glance at the directions. When, however, the computer was then programmed, he acted as if in the presence of a nuclear meltdown and could not be induced to touch or go near the system. Not surprisingly, he treated everything she produced for him on the p.c. (particularly if it included words in bold or underscored) with something approaching awe (*see* Abilities: Letter Writing and Work/Hers: Writing).

Cooking: *See* Cookery: all categories.

Do-It-Yourself (D.I.Y.): More than once, she'd silently replaced his true initials with these three. His matter-of-fact attitude toward decoration and/or construction of items for both house and garden was a revelation to one whose father *and* stepfather could not change a lightbulb without outside assistance. Barring certain kinds of rewiring and plumbing, there seemed nothing he couldn't do. Spirited participation in most of these jobs inevitably developed some rudimentary skills on her part. She was praised more than once for her proficiency at painting walls, knocking in rawl plugs, holding pieces of wood he was cutting, and marking off where the book shelves had to go. Perhaps the one stumbling block in her D.I.Y. mastery was the use of power tools, which no amount of persuasion could get her to operate (*see* Garden: various; House: various; and Passions/Cinema: Cinema).

Finances: Though no more proficient in mathematics than he, she nevertheless conveyed an inborn *je ne sais quoi* as regards the mechanics of bill paying and collecting of monies owed that convinced him to leave such matters in her hands. That said, they always discussed and mutually agreed on all expenditures and it is *he* who must be given credit for the idea of a daily expense list to show exactly how much was spent by the pair on a quarterly basis (*see* Character: Practicality and Money: Budget).

Healing: Among all the skills he possessed, a power to heal was the only one she didn't learn of prior to the occasion when the need for it arose. Around their first Christmas, she developed a sort of cyst in the inside of her lower lip, which very soon discoloured the corresponding visible area. Certain that a salve or balm could cure the problem, she was dismayed to hear her G.P. announce that surgical removal was the only solution, and that it would be several months before that could be arranged. He initially seemed as dismayed as she, and so it was a surprise when that very same evening, he offered to lay hands on her lip. Nevertheless, she agreed and he continued the practice (sometimes several times a day) for about ten days, when the discolouration definitely began to fade. Soon it was gone, and with it the cyst. She then learned that the healing was limited (it didn't work on himself, for example, or with every complaint), but such details did not stop her offering his services soon after to a mutual friend at whose house they were dining and who was suffering from severe toothache. Embarrassed at being called upon and continually protesting that he couldn't always help, he in fact succeeded in relieving the friend's pain until 4:00 P.M. the following afternoon (*see* Character: Self-effacement).

Letter writing: Being a writer, correspondence of any sort was a simple business for her. Even before the purchase of the magic p.c., she could always produce a letter in under twenty minutes and be pleased with the result. He, on the other hand, wrestled mightily with even the simplest note. Very early on, she offered to write all their business letters, and he gratefully accepted. He then asked her to look at his personal letters as well—a job she accepted with trepidation as she knew she was quite capable of getting carried away and rewriting them in her own words. The few times when her vigilance failed and that happened he said nothing, but simply went back to the original text in his fair copy—which he also showed her (*see* Self-image/Contributing to: Literacy).

Photography: Not counting the things she had never tried, perhaps the greatest gap in their respective skills lay in photography. She had little idea of what taking pictures involved and less about cameras. He, on the other hand, owned several cameras and knew their every feature; he could talk intelligently in a photographic shop and set up all shots with a thoroughness that prompted her (if she wasn't the subject) to wander off after a time. All the same, she did have a single experience as a true photographer during their time together. About six months before he died, he decided to produce slides of his recent paintings and drawings and asked her to help him. This involved going together to buy lighting equipment; draping the background material; moving lights and umbrellas around for each shot; noting down what exposures were for what pictures; and finally reviewing the results with him when they were ready (*see* Art/Summary and Love/Summary).

Sewing: While the proficiency of both of them viz. sewing was not monumental, he could use a sewing machine (she'd never learned) and had had the courage to create the loose cover patterns for their car, Mini the Moocher. Pattern or no, the four words "time to machine it" heralded a ritual that never varied. First, he'd carry in the sewing machine, an object that weighed as much as himself. He'd then study the directions and say: "It's been so long since I've used this thing last, I can't remember how it works." Next emerged the bobbin that was invariably wound into a sort of Gordian knot, which she unsnarled—only too glad to be doing something. After that (and most tumultuous) was the threading of the needle. This could not be effected until he'd (a) cursed like a sailor for a minimum of 15 minutes; (b) told her to go out to buy more thread because he was rapidly using up the colour; (c) again consulted the directions; and (d) finally announced that the machine was just too old to be of any use. Just at the point of her asking if it wouldn't be simpler doing it by hand, the needle finally picked up the thread from the bobbin, and he'd proceed to the job. The reference to hand sewing, incidentally, was not an idle one, as it was she who replaced all buttons and put patches on his jeans when the holes got too big.

Spelling: His spelling was so atrocious that at times she would mentally review the reasons why the ability to spell was so valued— English spelling hadn't been standardised before Dr. Johnson; *content* was what mattered, dictionaries existed specifically to deal with the other—things like that. She never said any of this to him, however, aware that it was a delicate subject. It was simpler to become his living dictionary—a service that suited him so well it became his rule to consult her for his own information as well as for private and public communications (*see* Abilities: Letter writing and Self-image/Contributing to: Literacy).

Art

Summary

By training, he was a painter and sculptor. Given the esteem she ultimately developed for his very real talent in both mediums, it amused her to recall that she'd been dismissive the first time she'd seen his work. At that particular exhibition, none of his sculptures or drawings had been on view, and his paintings had disturbed her by their subject matter (e.g., acres of sumo wrestlers and angst-ridden abstracts). During their time together, his own view of his talents never varied. He passionately felt he was still learning as a painter (he had been a sculptor most of his life); was never satisfied with a finished work; or if (in an unguarded moment) did admit that a painting "wasn't bad," would always quickly add that he couldn't believe he'd done it. He'd exhibited a fair amount over the years and once (briefly) had been able to earn his living as an artist. Nevertheless, when he began sending out slides of his most recent work, he gently explained to her that he'd probably have to try a number of galleries before one showed interest, so she shouldn't be disappointed if this first lot all sent back rejections. He was wrong. One of the first lot *did* accept him, but as he died before the letter was received, she couldn't be sure the news reached him (*see* Abilities: Photography; Art/Concepts: all categories; Beliefs: Afterlife; Passions/Art: various; and Work/Summary; Work/His: Animation).

Concepts

Imagination: She knew *he* knew the rules of the art world, namely, to establish one's reputation it was necessary to build up a large body of work in the same style. She also knew he couldn't bring himself to do it. His imagination was too far-reaching and compelling. He would always yield to a new idea without seeing the previous one through to the completion he had first envisioned. Her feelings about this were mixed. Since he *wanted* a reputation, it was unfortunate. On the other hand, his delight in each new project was so profound, she couldn't help but share it and be thrilled at the result. At the end of his life, ideas simply poured from him. During his first stay in hospital, she was constantly bringing him art materials. He drew and painted continuously. Likewise when he came home—as long as his strength held out. His very last project was a series of "aura" portraits. This would have involved life-sized tracing of the subject and then filling in the space with whatever colours the subject's aura suggested. He wrote about the idea to a painter friend in New York and included sample 5″ by 7″ sketches. He even managed to trace her standing in the nude, but then became too ill to progress further. His final inability to work at all was, in her eyes, as much a death as his actual passing (*see* Illness/Last [His]/Experiences: Hospital; Work/Summary; and Art: Figure 1).

Figure 1: A projected "aura"

Imitation: The influence of his three heroes, Bacon, Klee, and Van Gogh (and a nonhero, Munch), was often apparent in his paintings, much as the style of Giacometti had been in his earliest sculptures. He was barely aware of the borrowing; she, though more aware, yet understood that his own interior vision discounted the possibility of him ever producing pastiche (*see* Biography/Joint: Guggenheim and Passions/Art: various).

Incubation: As a couple, they exhibited radically different work strategies. She was a plodder. Day after day, she'd either do research for or commit to paper some dialogue for an intended play. That the research was occasionally gratuitous or the dialogue woeful counted little: it gave her an illusion of working. He, on the other hand, genuinely required an incubation period for an idea. At such times, not even a sketch emerged from his pen. While he saw no difference in her pretend work and his cogitation, she couldn't see why he was wasting time. Again and again, he felt called upon to assure her that he *was* working and to prove it by doodling something for her benefit. When at last she did come to understand, she was dismayed at her meanness in not having trusted him (*see* Love/General: Trust and Work/Hers: Writing).

Modern art: The couple agreed in the main about the practitioners of modern art. His heroes were also hers, with the exception of Bacon, whom she admired rather than liked—much as she tried (for his sake) to do both—and Matisse, whom she couldn't stomach at all. Both tended to question art that evidenced no sign of an ability (in some form) to draw, paint, or sculpt. Both enjoyed going to exhibitions of modern art—she, unreservedly; he, when his mind didn't have to be absolutely clear for a picture he was working on. She was content to let her involvement with modern art be confined to attending galleries and museums and perhaps watching the odd informative programme on television. He supplemented these activities by reading and rereading art magazines with as much zest as she did a good novel (*see* Concepts: Imitation and Passions/Art: various).

E LEMENTS

Light: A certain light emanated from his paintings and drawings. It appeared to come directly from artist to subject irrespective of any depicted light, and it struck her every time she saw it. Whether *he* was conscious of the light, she could only speculate. He tended to be overly critical of his own work and might well have looked at her with astonishment had she brought it to his attention. That notwithstanding, "personal light" constituted a vital part of her very own labouriously evolved theory concerning the power of his art (*see* Art/Summary).

Line: He was an absolute master of cross-hatching. During their time together, she would watch him take pencil or pen, turn the paper virtually black with lines, and finally conclude that he had started an idea, got it wrong, and in frustration was just doodling to fill up the page. But when he then *showed* her the "doodles," what she would see were unearthly night scenes or stark figures emerging out of layers of shadow upon shadow. With coloured pencils or pastels, he could and did produce everything from ethereal landscapes to Munch-like unfortunates. His patience in getting the cross-hatching right was extraordinary. Six to seven hours was not uncommon in producing a picture no more than 4″ by 4″ (*see* Art/Materials: various and Art: Figure 2).

Primary colours: He had a definite preference for tracks of red, yellow, and blue in his paintings—above all in portraits and abstracts where he was free to use his imagination as to subject or background. He had, more than once, told her he was colour-blind, which, given the stunning colour combinations he could produce when he wanted to, she at first had found hard to credit. Upon reflection, however, she began to wonder if the importance primary colours held for him didn't in fact indicate some degree of colour-blindness on his part.

Proportion: Though he was a more than competent draughtsman, classical proportion sometimes figured in his work as a tenet to violate. In certain portraits, for example, a disproportion between head and body was used as one means of depicting the inner character of the individual. In other work, where colour or brush stroke was the key feature, he would mathematically calculate the proportions of certain background features (she only had to think of his painstakingly depicted checkered floors or blown-up dotted carpets sloping off into a narrowing horizon). While she saw with her own eyes that deliberately flouting the rules of proportion could be an effective device in a picture, she also knew that when it failed, the results were inevitably grim (*see* Art/Styles: various).

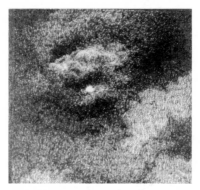

Figure 2: Cross-hatching

Scale: His oil and acrylic paintings (though there was also one monster in pastels) tended to be over-large, when his drawings and some sculptures weren't. She privately felt that his inclination to the grand scale in this medium was the second jewel in the crown of his disdain for the art world. He probably would have denied that theory and substituted one about quality more than compensating for something as trivial as size. Still, he wasn't totally insensitive to practicalities—as was demonstrated the one time they'd contemplated a local one-man exhibition of his paintings. The issue of invitations arose. He remarked he was happy just inviting their friends; she remarked that while friends were all very well, if he actually wanted to *sell* the pictures, it might do to invite those with access to walls large enough to hang them, namely, college and corporation representatives and denizens of the city's more exclusive neighbourhoods. He'd not disagreed (*see* Art/Concepts: Imagination).

FORM

Drawing: His drawings were done singly or in series. They had two functions: to be seen in their own right or to serve as models for paintings or sculpture. The first and second functions could overlap and (very occasionally) give way to a third—the practice sketch. Unlike his American painter friend who tried to do at least one sketch a day to keep his eye sharp (and contrary even to his own pronouncements that this or that drawing was the herald of the same policy for himself), these were always one-off. This really didn't surprise her. She knew him well enough to understand that discipline—while important once he was actually working—had far less value as a source of inspiration.

Painting: Living with him, she came to appreciate what it meant to be a painter. Before ever taking up a brush, he'd laboriously prepare his surfaces and lament over having to spend a morning buying colours and/or brushes that he lacked. Once the picture was underway, he'd explain to her that he daren't risk even going to the loo because the paints might dry and he'd have to start again (though she didn't completely understand this). When he'd paint over errors, he'd stand there and *will* the paints to dry because he couldn't proceed while they were wet. Even finishing the painting wasn't the end: there was still the varnishing and framing to be done. It seemed to her that what pushed him along were the materials: preparing them, buying them, drying them, and eternally worrying over them. Not unnaturally, she compared it to her own situation. Would she write one single word if she had to programme the bloody p.c. every time she sat down? At times she felt like asking him how *he* managed, how the sheer donkey work didn't dry up his inspiration entirely. But then she'd look at the completed picture and decide it was a silly question.

Sculpture: He had "officially" given up sculpture some four years before they'd met and only dabbled at two or three small pieces during their time together. So it was that, unlike drawing or painting, his working method as a sculptor was closed to her. Even her appreciation of existing pieces had to wait until after his death as *he* had displayed little interest in them, preferring to hide the lot in a back corner of their shed. Her joy at the ingenuity and beauty of the pieces (the majority ranked alongside his best paintings and drawings) was soured only by not being able to tell him what she thought. The style of the sculpture (almost all in one or another kind of wood or reinforced resin) varied substantially from his two-dimensional work. In explanations written for past exhibitions, he had called the work earth and/ or disintegration forms. In her opinion, the pieces were visceral-looking—literally—and pointed to an intense sensuality (*see* Art/Summary/Materials: Wood; Passions/Art: Wood; and Work/His: Carpentry).

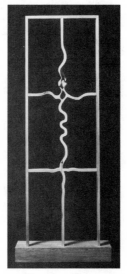

Figure 3: Wood sculpture

MATERIALS

Acrylics: Though he hadn't spoken of using acrylics in the past (and she was too ignorant to know simply by looking), during their time together the latter were the chief medium for everything he painted. Their ability to dry quickly was a relative one and, sadly, a virtue unmatched either by a less powerful odour than oils (at least to her nose) or a particularly cheap price (*see* Art/Form: Painting and Art/Materials: Oils).

Board: All his paintings tended to be on chipboard—he claimed it was easier and less dear than canvas (though he'd planned to use canvas for his "aura" paintings). Every few months, he would order an enormous board (cut down into the sizes he stipulated) from a building materials merchant and whitewash the lot so each was ready when needed. An unlooked-for benefit with the chipboard was that together they were able to devise a painted frame, a white border of seven eighths of an inch surrounded by a black border about three times in width (*see* Materials: Canvas).

Brushes: He had no less than fifty brushes, ranging from a few thin hairs to some that could, at a pinch, be used for D.I.Y. Though he had explained to her that sable ones were the best (being the longest lasting), the proportion of them in his total stock was small as a result of their fabulous price and because he might have had qualms over using the fur (*see* Abilities: Do-It-Yourself and Biography/Joint: Sable).

Canvas: Visiting innumerable art-supply shops with him, she'd repeatedly seen other artists purchasing canvas and the equipment to stretch it with. The whole process seemed to her even more tedious and delaying than whitewashing chipboard, and she was grateful he had—at least until the projected "aura" pictures—rejected it as a surface (*see* Art/Concepts: Imagination and Art/Materials: Board).

Clay: She couldn't recall the circumstances of the purchase—perhaps he had received a catalogue from somewhere or the fancy had just taken him. Whichever, one day clay sufficient to supply every crafts course in the south of England arrived and took up residence in his studio. And there (saving two very small, unfinished pieces begun in the last weeks of his life) it remained (*see* Art/Form: Sculpture).

Coloured pencils: Before meeting him, she'd always considered coloured pencils as something for children. His extraordinary drawings in the medium changed her mind irrevocably. In his patient hand, they became as expressive as acrylics or oils. More than that, they were user-friendly. They required no preparation and little cleanup; they didn't have to dry and at no point did they smell (*see* Art/Elements: Line and Art/Subjects: Cityscape, Rockets).

Gouache: He'd done only a few small pictures in gouache, chiefly when the couple had been in New York City. Though they came in tubes unlike watercolours, she still tended to confuse the two as he used water with both. Her confusion usually vanished, however, upon seeing the finished work (*see* Art/Subjects: Landscapes and Biography/Joint: Travel).

Hand tools: The impressive number of these he possessed were to do chiefly with sculpture. As he'd never explained the function of any of them or used them more than twice during their time together, she could only surmise as to the particular purpose of each. She *had* observed that they were useful with both plaster of Paris and clay, and some were intended to hack off unwanted bits whereas others were for scraping or polishing. Beyond that, they all looked like a set of dental instruments for someone with exceedingly large teeth (*see* Art/Form: Sculpture and Art/Materials: Clay, Plaster of Paris).

Oils: Though the first picture he'd painted during their time together had been in oils, he had abandoned them as a medium immediately thereafter, telling her that they took too long to dry. The decision was not an easy one, as a part of him firmly believed that oils were superior to acrylics. That notwithstanding (and to her surprise, given all the other bother he went to), it was a belief he resolutely suppressed in favour of convenience (*see* Art/Form: Painting and Art/Materials: Acrylics).

Pastels: He did nothing in pastels while she knew him, though there were several completed and framed drawings from several years earlier. Just after his death, one of these was chosen (along with works in other mediums) for an exhibition at a local gallery. The gallery manager showed her the smudge marks the pastels had made on the white matte surrounding the picture. Apparently, pastels required a fixative, which he had either forgotten or chosen not to use. Unable to ask him *why* he hadn't, she contented herself with mentally fixing pastels (on a scale of mess) halfway between acrylics and coloured pencils.

Pen and ink: *See* Art/Elements: Line.

Pencil: *See* Art/Elements: Line.

Plaster of Paris: In her mind, there was an inextricable connection between plaster of Paris and clay. For some reason, both had become the materials in which he sculpted; both were purchased in such exorbitant quantity that it had required the two of them to haul the container bags indoors; and both remained largely unused. That said, the earth-mother statuette he'd done in plaster of Paris was finished as far as modelling and simply waited to be painted, whereas illness had prevented him from proceeding beyond the very first stages with his two maquettes in clay (*see* Art/Form: Sculpture and Art/Materials: Clay, Hand tools).

Varnish: Unlike pastels, whose decaying possibilities hadn't overly concerned him, he was *very* aware of having to protect his paintings and agonised over the correct varnish to use. As far as she could gather, they were either water based or something-else based, and the wrong one could discolour the work. It was necessary, therefore, to try different ones on corners of a painting to see what happened. She recalled him doing so on one or two pictures, deciding *a* was better than *b* but, at the end of it, still leaving most of the newer work unprotected (*see* Art/Materials: Pastels).

Watercolours: She had a soft spot for watercolours. Had fate blessed her with artistic ability, it was undoubtedly the medium she would have worked in. She never once told him of this preference. *He* seemed to value them for their ease of use—they didn't require a studio or even tubes to carry them in. The twice he'd used them were both times away from home: on the cliffs near Swanage and during his time in hospital (*see* Art/Subjects: Landscape and Illness/Last [His]/Experiences: Hospital).

Wood: In her eyes his ability with wood was phenomenal. He could and did do anything with it: tie it into knots, twist it into elastic curves, pare it to the thickness of a feuille or create shapes that resembled viscera or occasionally molten glass. Everyone who saw the work was drawn to touch it. He had made no mention of touching in his notes, and she'd decided to interpret the omission as assent (*see* Art/Form: Sculpture; Passions/Art: Wood; and Work/His: Carpentry).

STYLES

Experimental: Experimentation was a major part of his work. The particular forms he created through his sculpture were unique. His paintings and drawings tended to be more conventional, though there were a number of abstracts whose subject matter seemed to have been dredged up from the dark side of his unconscious and committed raw to the paper or board. Indeed, their particular brew of horror, sensuality, and despair had profoundly disturbed her and rendered her incapable of forming a reasonable judgment as to their merit (*see* Art/Summary/Elements: Proportion).

Representational: Over his artistic life, he'd drawn and painted portraits, landscapes, cityscapes, and objects. While quite able to capture any and all subjects with accuracy, his inner vision usually (though not inevitably) prompted him to invest pictures with a sense of pathos and/or mystery that went beyond it. During their time together, she became aware that however often his own inner vision might fail him, it never moderated his contempt for artists who merely reproduced what they saw (*see* Art/Summary/Elements: Proportion and Art/Subjects: various).

SUBJECTS

Abstract: *See* Art/Summary/Styles: Experimental.

Cityscape: A great deal of his time during their visit to New York City in 1993 was spent on the balcony of her mother's flat, sketching views of lower Manhattan. He completed a total of eleven coloured-pencil drawings in all, six of which made up a series that were later reproduced as oil or acrylic paintings. Occasional forays off the balcony also proved fruitful: four drawings of New York City street scenes were added to the collection before they left (*see* Art/Materials: various and Biography/Joint: New York City).

Landscape: With the exception of a handful of watercolours from the cliffs near Swanage, all of his landscapes were done prior to their relationship. They depicted American locations (in particular, a very beautiful island off the Maine coast) and were limited to pencil or coloured pencils. Unlike the New York cityscapes, they don't seem to have been intended as the prototypes for any sort of paintings (*see* Art/Materials: Watercolours; Subjects: Cityscape; and Art: Figure 4).

Portraiture: His portraits were uncanny. Regardless of medium or when completed, they invariably captured the soul rather than a

Figure 4: A landscape

physical likeness. The subject of one portrait (upon first viewing) uttered an expletive, gazed at it in silence for what seemed a full three minutes, and then turned around and announced that the man in the picture needed therapy. While she couldn't guess what *he* had made of that reaction, to her it had been the ultimate praise.

Rockets: After his death, she had come upon four coloured-pencil drawings of rockets as they might be seen falling onto the country-side from above. The drawings had puzzled her until she remembered that his house had received a direct rocket hit during World War II. Her thesis was confirmed when, after his death, she came upon a memoir he had written of the event (*see* Art/Materials: Coloured pencils and Biography/His: Rockets).

Self-portraiture: His three self-portraits left no doubt in her mind that he was probably more devastatingly honest with himself than anyone else he painted, his own mix of vulnerability and sweetness speaking unequivocally in two of the pictures and peeking through the third (*see* Abilities/Summary; Art/Summary/Elements: Light; and Character: Diffidence).

Sumo wrestling: *See* Passions/Japan: all categories.

*A*ttitudes

Summary

The attitudes of the pair were sufficiently alike to count as a decisive factor in their affection. As she well knew how bizarre her attitudes happened to be, at first she couldn't quite believe it and had wondered if he wasn't just *saying* he agreed out of (a) love, (b) natural amenability, (c) a desire for peace, or (d) all of the preceding. He soon cured her of that notion, however, by challenging a few cherished attitudes in a manner that rendered both intricate reasoning and bombast ineffectual. As to changing *her* mind, it wasn't in his nature to try (*see* Love: various).

Children: Neither of them planned on having or wanted children. He had a grown daughter and for various reasons, she'd always had little desire for motherhood. The one time she thought she might be pregnant, the pair had gone to the family planning clinic with urine at the ready. The doctor's remark, "I'm afraid I have bad news" had in fact presaged an announcement that the result was negative. She'd instantly taken offence and was on the point of launching into her "doomed planet" spiel when he'd whispered into her ear to let well enough alone and manoeuvred her out of the office (*see* Attitudes: Ecology, Population; Character: Heroism; and Work/Hers: Writing).

Ecology: She talked green; he lived it, raising his own fruits and vegetables and building much of what he required. Differences in practice notwithstanding, they were united in the idea that the earth was likely headed for some sort of environmental disaster within the next generation. Her worry over the future did not survive the trauma of his death (*see* Abilities: Do-It-Yourself; Attitudes: Politics, Population; Character: Heroism; Garden/Summary: various; House/Summary: various; and Work/His: Carpentry, Joinery).

Health maintenance: Each had his own way of maintaining general health: she attended Keep Fit classes once a week while he sporadically did body-building exercises. The equipment lying around the house at such times had intrigued her, and, somewhat pleased, he devised what he regarded as a gentle routine for her to follow. This was not a success. Keep Fit notwithstanding, she had difficulty lifting the smallest weights and at each attempt only managed to get through what she was supposed to by enduring considerable pain (*see* Character: Laziness; Love/General: Monogamy; and Self-image/Contributing to: Muscle).

Hiking: He possessed the natural love of walking that came with a childhood in the countryside. She had a New Yorker's dread of treading on anything that wasn't concrete and absolutely flat. During the few mini-walks attempted around their home in the country, she'd found herself a constant prey of ditches, low-lying branches, and turds of all descriptions, whereas he'd happily loped along. When she asked to be excused from future walks, he replied that all she needed were the proper shoes and a pair of Dr. Marten's were duly purchased for her. In fact, they'd made little difference (*see* Biography/Joint: Walks).

Marriage: His offers to marry her if she really wanted him to (and her repeated assurance that she didn't) served as love statements rather than a serious topic of discussion between the pair, as neither believed it was possible to be more committed as a couple than they already were. From their very first weeks together, they'd found that persons who dealt with them as householders usually assumed they were married and addressed them as such. While neither ever bothered to correct this impression, each one did think it important to ask the other's pardon every time they didn't (*see* Love/Summary/ General: Anniversaries and Time: Years).

Pacificism: Her advocacy of pacificism was *the* example of an attitude she could not convince him of. He held the traditional view that war was a ghastly business but unavoidable when one's home and loved ones were attacked. She believed that a highly organised form of social defence and noncooperation was as effective as combat in ultimately undermining an invader and cited instances proving her point. He'd been impressed, but still maintained that her system would never work on a large scale and, anyway, it had no chance of being adopted (*see* Attitudes/Summary).

Politics: A hearty loathing of mainstream politics (not to mention politicians) had resulted in two strains of behaviour in the pair. He refrained from political work altogether; she had joined a marginal party that represented her green point of view. Soon after their first meeting, her party had polled their largest vote ever in a local election. Soon after *that,* he became a party member, distributing leaflets, even helping at one or two fund-raising events. Never one to throw aside conceit, she decided that burgeoning affection was more likely the reason for this activity than any realization of what party politics could achieve (*see* Biography/Joint: Meeting, first).

Population: A corollary of impending environmental disaster was the "too many people" theory (overpopulation being as likely to do in the planet as pollution). Indeed, one caused the other, particularly if even a small proportion of that too many were Westerners like themselves. It was a theory they both shared, though he advanced it with far more circumspection—feeling, perhaps, that begetting a child of his own deprived him of the privilege of enthusiasm (*see* Attitudes: Children, Ecology).

Rain: Like all true Englishmen, he had bitterly resented extended periods of cold, rainy weather. Each time one occurred, he'd curse

England with a vehemence only surpassed by his language toward the sewing machine and ask himself why on earth he went on living here. Not so with her. Having *chosen* to live in England (instead of Bermuda or Hawaii, say) she always felt complaints were inappropriate. Indeed, she had generally proffered no opinion whatsoever (*see* Abilities: Sewing and Attitudes: Snow).

Snow: In a quasi-reversal of their attitudes toward rain, he had absolutely adored snow and she had as absolutely loathed it. Granted, she wasn't insensible to beautiful white landscapes or intense stillness—as her admiration for the occasional hoarfrost attested to. Perhaps if snowfall could somehow have been confined to areas of winter sports or human contemplation, she would have been as big a fan. Given, however, that (a) it wasn't, (b) what did fall often turned to black slush or ice, and (c) black or white, too much of the stuff was synonymous with injury, cabin fever, and even animal starvation, she could only conclude that his longing for it was downright selfish (*see* Attitudes: Hiking, Rain and Biography/Joint: Walks).

Women: His attitude toward women had been a revelation. He seemed totally devoid of male chauvinism, as if something or someone had stripped it from him or somehow it had never developed in the first place. At first she had felt this too good to be true. She even wondered if it might just be a pose but then concluded that he wasn't the type to impress. Their time together didn't prove her wrong (*see* Love/Summary/General: Monogamy; Love/Specific: Caressing; and Sex/Considerations: Pleasure).

B

....

Beliefs

Summary
Throughout her life, she'd accumulated a store of beliefs. He hadn't. Or else he had, but then decided that most of them were too woolly to merit discussion. Whenever she'd delved into her own store, he'd listened with an attentiveness that had convinced her he was just waiting for the chance to tell her what he thought. It was inevitably an illusion. Not only had he generally little to say, but once or twice extracting any comment at all from him had proved a heavy undertaking.

Afterlife: Had either of them ever guessed what a relevant topic this was destined to become, they might have devoted more attention to it. As it was, beyond mutually rejecting notions of angels, harps, clouds, wings, and all the other paraphernalia of heaven (hell had never reached the starting line of consideration), but allowing that the spirit continued in *some* form after death, the two were fairly vague. His own death clarified a great deal. Some hours after he'd expired, his face had briefly appeared to her: He was smiling sheepishly, as if sorry to have caused so much fuss. She was impressed that he'd managed to get through and had informed him he had nothing to be sorry about. A few weeks later, while watching a video of a Chinese film, she'd semi-dozed and seen him prancing around to the music accompanying the film. Unlike the first visit, all signs of his terrible illness had disappeared. His presence in the room was so powerful, upon opening her eyes she'd been surprised to find that she was alone. Both events had persuaded her that though she couldn't actually summon him, in some way he was hanging around (*see* Illness/Last [His]: various and Love/Specific: Laughter).

Apocalypticism: *See* Attitudes: Children, Ecology, Population.

God: Both of them had been surprised to learn that quite independently, each had hit upon a definition of God as a universal mind that both animated and influenced all things. Such a definition did not insult one's intelligence by positing a bearded, bad-tempered old man in the sky *or* bruise one's soul by insisting on nothing at all. After his death, however, when grief had reduced her to spluttering rage and vows of undying hatred for the terrible and repeated anguish that had been visited upon her, she found herself directing them at a deity in human form. Even allowing (in her saner moments) that there was no reason for the universal mind not to have a dark side, it was ultimately more satisfying to have the God of the Old Testament as a metaphysical punching bag (*see* Beliefs: Religion; Biography/Hers: various; Biography/Joint: Seders; and Passions/Holidays: all categories).

Immortality: About six weeks before they'd met, she offered the universal mind the following proposition: If somehow it wasn't her lot to have immortality as a writer *and* great love, might she have just one? It didn't matter which. The latter apparently granted, it hadn't been difficult to redirect her own desire for immortality to a desire for his. As far as she knew (a) he wasn't under her constraints; (b) he wished it, and (c) when she honestly compared his talent as an artist to hers as a writer, she concluded he deserved it more than herself. But then he'd died, and she could not throw off the chilling thought that perhaps she was being set up to have *both* her wishes, only one after the other (*see* Art/Summary; Biography/Joint: New York City; and Work/Summary).

Miracles: Though the two had shared a belief in the possibility of miracles (ranging on a scale from "Just Possible" at the top end to "Never in a Million Years" at the bottom), the reasons *why* they had varied. She felt the new physics made it impossible to dismiss nonscientific phenomenon out-of-hand. He was less interested in specific explanations than in the documentaries and/or discussions he saw or heard on radio or television—as if treatment by the media automatically conferred credibility. Perhaps the single miracle the two acknowledged as existing outside explanation was finding each other and falling in love—though admittedly, the latter did not contravene natural law (*see* Character: Youthfulness and Love: various).

Pantheism: *See* Beliefs: God.

Reincarnation: During their entire time together, she'd been unable to draw him into a single discussion concerning reincarnation. Though in one sense it had been a disappointment, in another it had been a relief in that his lack of interest had allowed her the luxury of not having to try and explain that what she *termed* reincarnation was actually lazy shorthand for *simultaneous incarnation*. This was a system whereby *all* one's lives happened at the same time and were on tap, so to speak, for the soul to choose from—which it did by adhering to one much as a ship followed a single lane at sea (*see* Illness/Chronic: Epilepsy).

Religion: While the couple had both been soured on their respective religions in childhood, the resultant behaviour had not been parallel. He considered the Church of England as beneath even the dignity of a mention; she was only too happy to launch into a bitter critique of Judaism at the smallest pretext. As to religions other than their own, whenever the pair entered places of worship as visitors, she always discreetly said a prayer or two, imagining the universal mind to be the core of all religions, so why not. He, on the other hand, usually just wandered around, sketched anything he thought looked interesting, and then indicated that it was time to move on (*see* Beliefs: God; Biography/Hers: various; Biography/Joint: Seders; Cookery/Specialties [His]: Pancakes; and Passions/Holidays: various).

Soul: When the pair spoke at all about the soul, it was usually as a synonym for spirit. Wider usage was generally avoided, as both instinctively knew that the latter might, at some point, provoke investigation as to what and where the soul actually was—always a recipe for disaster (*see* Beliefs: Afterlife).

Spirituality: That the two had their own brand of spirituality was plainly evidenced by (a) a mutual acceptance of both the universal mind and the continuation of the spirit after death, (b) a mutual integrity that invalidated ruthlessness as a stratagem, (c) a readiness (even to the detriment of their own work) to help out both friends and family, and (d) his healing powers (*see* Abilities: Healing; Beliefs: Afterlife, God; Character: various; and Work/Summary).

*B*iography

Summary

She was forty-eight and he fifty-six years old, respectively, when they met. They had lived in the same area for over twenty years without knowing of each other's existence, and some ten years prior to being introduced had experienced the end of important relationships in both their lives: him, through divorce and her (as would happen again), through death. Both had sought other partners, but never with particular success so that much of the intervening period had been difficult. As the years passed, both had become increasingly convinced that they were destined to spend the rest of their lives alone. Certainly, neither was prepared for what happened when they finally *did* meet. Their attraction to each other was immediate and their affection very soon declared. Once begun, their life together was marked by interdependence to an uncanny degree and the ability to spend any amount of time in the other's company without adverse effect (*see* Abilities/Summary; Beliefs: God; Biography/Joint: Attraction [mutual]; and Love: all categories).

Hers

America: She'd been born and raised in the United States, but sore disillusionment had prompted her to move to England in 1973. Once *in* England, however, her nationality became a valuable asset. People liked her accent and her directness, and the presence of hordes of her compatriots over the years had not seemed to change their minds. Being an American had particularly worked to her advantage in relationships. It had been part of her mystique for her first great love and as for *him*—a preference for women from the other side of the ocean was more than attested to by the American nationality of all the women he had ever loved. (*see* Biography/ Summary/Hers: Jew; Biography/Joint: Greece [Thassos], Voice; Money: Dollar; and Wills: Estates).

Delicatessen: "Delicatessen" cuisine was a feature of her past that she badly missed. It seemed to exist only in London (where they didn't live), and so was not available to her for many years. Even after a cold cut or two finally began to put in a local appearance, there was pathetically little to choose from, and it never tasted as authentic as home. During their time in New York City, she'd taken him to her favourite deli, but he'd been more struck by her delight at again being able to eat her favourite dishes and the general ambience than by the food itself (*see* Biography/Joint: New York City).

Epilogue: Not merely his death from cancer, but having to watch him die of it had crushed her. God knows it had been bad enough with Love No. 1, who, despite knowing for four years, she hadn't *lived* with and who had died instantly from a heart attack and not in her presence. That fate could once again take the man she loved (and this time in circumstances 10,000 times more horrific) goaded her into a search for explanations. The first was astrological and came unsolicited. During a short stay in New York just after his death, a cousin compiled her chart and declared that a death planet had been with her for a number of years but was at last on the point of veering away (a theory subsequently confirmed by a professional astrologer). In England, a friend whose partner had left her after fifteen years offered her own theory about Earth being God's toilet. Personally (since she believed in simultaneous incarnation), she wondered if this life wasn't the payoff for a parallel fifty or so years as an arms dealer or the like. All other theories, however, involved God's vendetta against her. That the two deaths were unrelated events and that she'd simply had very bad luck (as her bereavement therapist insisted) she continued to find simplistic and unacceptable. A search for explanations was not her only food for thought in the months following his death. The entire experience had also (a) inclined her to the Buddhist notion of "living in the present" (with a future extending to this week and perhaps the next, but no further, (b) rendered her indifferent to illness, dying, or whatever catastrophes might be in store for the planet, (c) nullified (when *a* and *b* were taken together) the moral imperative that formerly had impelled her to work for peace and the green cause, and (d) caused her to be grateful he had been a creative artist, for promoting his work (whatever the results) seemed to make the days more livable (*see* Attitudes: Ecology; Beliefs: various; Biography/Hers: Job; Garden/Summary; House/Summary/Adventures: Shed; Illness/Last [His]: all categories; Love/General: Need; Money/Summary; Time/Summary; Transport: Public; Wills: Cremation; and Work/Summary).

Galicia: Her mother's family had come from Galicia, though she'd always been vague as to where it actually was and who it belonged to (her grandmother had spoken of her village changing hands several times). When her grandparents had emigrated to the United States at the beginning of the century, the authorities had listed them as Austrian, thus virtually insuring her mother's exclusion from meaningful war work some thirty-five years later. The single other fact she'd been able to tell him about Galicia was that *Galiziana* was a term of derision among Eastern European Jews.

Greens: *See* Attitudes: Ecology, Politics; Biography/Hers: Epilogue; and Character: Heroism.

Hungary: Her father's family had been Hungarian—her father having been born in Hungary and brought to the United States as a baby. Some years after their arrival, her grandmother had decided she didn't like America very much and had taken her father (though not her other children) back to the old country—supposedly for a visit. It had soon become obvious to her grandfather, however, that his wife had no intention of returning, and he'd gone to Hungary to retrieve her. An extraordinary thing then occurred. Her father was kidnapped by gypsies and held for three days before he was returned, and *that* apparently was sufficient to convince Grandmother that maybe America wasn't so bad after all. When she'd told him the story, he'd expressed disbelief at the kidnapping sequence. He'd merely wondered if her grandfather hadn't arranged it (*see* Biography/Joint: Grandmothers).

Jew: Soon after beginning her first year in school, the teacher had asked which children in the class were going to be out for the Jewish holidays. She hadn't raised her hand. The teacher gazed at her thoughtfully for a moment and then asked her to stand. The question was repeated. Very embarrassed, she replied she didn't know. The teacher then asked if she was Jewish and though she hadn't known that either, she was not about to say "I don't know" twice and desperately tried to think *what* she might be. At last deciding she was probably what she spoke, she announced she was

English, whereupon the teacher informed her that that was the wrong answer and to go home and ask her mother. Fair enough—that night before going to bed, she asked her mother if she was English and was told no, she was American. The following morning, she was again asked to stand. "Did you ask your mother, as I instructed?" asked the teacher, and she nodded. "Good. And are you Jewish?" to which she responded, "No, I'm American"—at which point the teacher told her not to worry, she'd send a note home. Years later, she would turn away from the Jewish religion because of a virulent sexism which, in her opinion, all the reformed groups in the world could never excise from its heart. Ethnically, there was no turning away, but she'd never wished to. In all her time in New York, that ethnicity had been taken for granted. In England (to her great surprise) it began to be celebrated. Gentile after gentile informed her that they'd never met a Jew who wasn't creative and intelligent—she could have introduced them to acres. And (along with being American) it could render her irresistible. He, for one, would stroke her dark curly hair with the sort of speechless wonder Rebecca had caused to flow in Ivanhoe's breast. It always reminded her of the time Love No. 1 had grown dewy-eyed at the end of the film version *Fiddler on the Roof* and (ignoring her protests that no one in her family came from Russia) solemnly declared that for the first time, he understood her roots (*see* Beliefs: God, Religion; Biography/Hers: various; and Self-image/Contributing to: Face).

Job (Bible): They had met in middle age, fallen in love, and found their ideal house. They'd laboured valiantly to decorate it in record time and had succeeded in creating work areas for themselves that were the envy of everyone who saw them. In his new freedom to paint full-time, he'd produced his best work to date and had ideas that would have kept him busy for many years to come. She had just completed the research for and was about to begin a new play on a subject dear to her heart. The relationship underpinning all of this was everything each had ever wanted: They were *the* loves of each other's lives. And then he'd fallen ill and within three months was dead. If all of that wasn't the outline for a modern version of Job, she couldn't imagine what else might be. Except this time it wasn't a question of renouncing God (her notion of a universal mind precluded, at least intellectually, notions of renunciation) but rather crushing what had been the best part of herself: her concern for the world and the future (*see* Attitudes/Summary: Ecology, Marriage; Biography/Summary; and Biography/Hers: Epilogue).

Menstruation: One day when she was about seven, she witnessed the girl next door being gently tapped on the face by various women in the neighbourhood. She'd asked her mother what was going on and was told that *x* had got her period for the first time, and doing that brought the blood back to her cheeks. She'd then asked her mother what a period was, thereby causing her mother to break into a sweat, as answering questions about menstruation was dangerously near to explaining about sex, a subject both her parents had rather hoped she would learn by osmosis. Her mother then promised she would tell her another time, and true to her word, several weeks later regaled her with a definition she'd memorised verbatim from a medical dictionary. The definition was so long and technical her mother could not actually stop before the end without instant memory wipeout, and all interruptions were met with, "Just let me finish first." After what seemed like hours, her mother at last indicated that she could now speak, and did she have any questions. She answered yes, only one: "Is the egg hard-boiled or soft-boiled?" She'd subsequently acquired a proper explanation while attending summer camp (*see* Illness/Chronic: Allergy and Sex/Considerations: Menstruation).

New York City: Her attitude toward her native city was ambivalent. She'd left it two decades earlier because she'd felt it was no longer a fit place in which to live. While visits over the years had not changed her mind, she'd always had to admit it was an exciting place. This was especially evident during their stay in 1993. Though he'd been to New York twice before, neither time had it been long enough for the city to work its full magic. Now it did, and she soon found herself sharing the enchantment. *That* New York (the city with everything on offer in large handfuls) was as much a reality as the other of poverty and crime, and however long she lived in England, she knew in a hundred different ways she would indelibly remain its product (*see* Attitudes: Hiking; Biography/Hers: various; Biography/Joint: New York City, Walks; Garden/Summary; House/Summary; and Passions: America, West, American).

Passover: Of all the Jewish holidays she ignored, Passover tended most to rattle her conscience—perhaps because she knew it went on for eight days and that by continuing to eat bread and the food she consumed all the rest of the year, every single day constituted a violation. Interestingly, Passover had not been observed in her home when she was a girl. Her mother, who'd seen the holiday as yet another excuse to heap unnecessary work on the religion's undeclared slaves, had refused to do anything about it beyond accepting invitations to other people's seders (*see* Beliefs: Religion; Biography/Hers: Jew; and Biography/Joint: Seders).

Quakers: Some months before meeting him, she'd experienced a craving for organised religion. As she had long admired the Society of Friends for their unswerving pacifism, she thought they might be the ones for her and so began to attend meetings. She was never able to feel a part of what was going on but probably would have persevered had they not then met. They did, however, and soon she had to admit that organised religion probably wasn't her thing, after all, and that there were other things she'd rather do on a Sunday morning (*see* Attitudes: Pacifism; Beliefs: Religion; and Sex/Realities: Erections).

Yiddish: Yiddish had not been spoken in her home, though her mother could and did converse in it with her grandmother. In New

York, her conversation would increasingly become peppered with Yiddish expressions to the extent that upon her return to England, for a week or two she'd find herself looking for an English phrase that expressed this or that idea as piquantly. During their time together, Yiddish had played enough of a role in her vocabulary for him to become familiar with a few simple words, though (unlike Love No. 1) he was never moved to try them himself (*see* Biography/Joint: Grandmothers).

HIS

Colouring, fair: When she'd met him, his hair and beard were a light blond—the first stage of a ginger-haired individual going grey. He told her that as a schoolboy his red hair had made him a figure of ridicule, an observation that astonished her every time she looked at coloured photographs of him as a younger man. His hair and beard had been a superb coppery auburn, the sort of colour American women paid out considerable sums of money to achieve (*see* Biography/His: School and Sex/Involving: Pubic Hair).

Cowboy: One of the first photos his mother had shown her was of him, aged about nine or ten, wearing a complete cowboy ensemble even down to hat and guns. She was somewhat surprised at the photo, having previously imagined the late 1940s as a bit early for cowboys to have entered the consciousness of English children (*see* Passions/America: West, American).

Crafts: The ability to make objects with his hands had been instilled in him by his father. By adulthood, it had become an integral part of his life, and (not surprisingly) during their time together he sought to teach her what he knew. Her resistance to his instruction, however, was unvarying, as she felt (if never actually stated) that the confidence needed for the *idea* of construction was acquirable only in one's childhood (*see* Abilities/Summary: Do-It-Yourself and Work/His: Carpentry, Joinery).

England: He'd been born in London and at about the time of his cowboy phase had moved with his family to the depths of Kent. That said, he never lost the city edge about him. As a New Yorker, she recognised it instantly, even if the city was not her own. His "London-ness" with its rural overlay played no small part in his initial attraction for her (*see* Biography/His: Cowboy, Rockets).

Kent: *See* England.

Leanness: Unlike hair colour, an attribute that he maintained from youth was leanness. The leanness seemed to be part of his build (as compared to svelteness achieved by exercise or diet) and was nothing he specifically worked at, though by nature he was an active man. At times, she silently compared his still muscular buttocks and thighs to her own and indulged in intense, if loving, envy. But then she learned that chronic stomach problems were perhaps as much a reason for his figure as anything else, and the leanness had lost some of its glamour (*see* Attitudes: Health maintenance; Biography/His: Walk; Illness/Last [His]/Symptoms: Weight loss; Love/General: Monogamy; and Self-image/Contributing to: Muscle).

Recession: Several years before they'd met, he had somehow acquired an American agent for his paintings. The agent not only managed to sell much of what he produced but had even paid him a weekly salary. The arrangement had continued until the United States recession in the eighties abruptly dried up the market and put the agent out of business (*see* Art/Summary and Work/Summary).

Rockets: When he was a baby during the war, the house he lived in with his parents, a set of grandparents, two aunts, and a dog received a direct hit from a V-2 rocket. Amazingly, all of them (down to the dog) escaped injury, though the house was more or less demolished. While he was never able to recall the actual explosion, he *did* vividly remember what remained of the family's furniture and other belongings being moved to a nearby house the following morning. After his death, she found four aerial views of rockets that he'd done in coloured pencil as well as a short written reflection on the experience (*see* Art/Subjects: Rockets and Self-image/Contributing to: Literacy).

School: School had been unremitting torment for him. He'd been neither a clever student nor a prodigious athlete, and his colouring had further marked him out as different. In an attempt to make his life bearable, his parents had sent him to different schools, but it was not until he was a teenager at art school that he at last found his niche and began to garner some morsels of self-respect. The scars left by his school experiences reached down to his very soul. No amount of love or admiration on her part ever totally erased his low self-esteem or the conviction that he was unable to learn (*see* Biography/His: Colouring, fair; Character: various; Love/General: Emergence; and Self-image/Contributing to: Learning, Literacy).

Self-reliance: *See* Abilities/Summary: Do-It-Yourself and Attitudes: Ecology.

Spain: As a young man—perhaps still in art school or just out of it— he'd spent a few months painting in Spain. While there, he and the student he'd gone with managed to run out of money to the extent of not eating for a few days, though the other bloke had managed, apparently, to save them from starvation. While he'd never go into detail as to *how,* apparently physical strength, raw wit, and a forceful personality—all of which the companion had possessed in abundance—had prominently figured. Indeed, he was usually more eager to talk about the bloke than tell her what she really wanted to know, namely, how (if at all) the sojourn had affected him as an artist.

Tepee: His involvement with tepees was both philosophical and practical. Philosophically, tepees represented simple living in its most desirable form. More than once, he'd proclaimed his disgust with houses and proposed the two of them give away everything and move into a large tepee only to hear her respond that *her* philosophy precluded even camping, never mind tepee-living. Practically, he and tepees went back many years. He'd actually sewn together an enormous twenty-foot tepee with the intention of using it in a business venture for his daughter. He'd also possessed a smaller version, which (in pre-*her* days) he'd used on various camping trips (*see* Abilities: Sewing and Attitudes: Hiking).

Vulnerability: *See* Abilities/Summary; Art/Summary/Elements: Light; Art/Subjects: Self-portraiture; Biography/His: Colouring, fair; Character: various; Love/General: Emergence; and Self-image/ Contributing to: Learning, Literacy.

Walk: He'd possessed a uniquely sexy walk. During their time together, she'd often gaze at him and try to analyze its components. One component, she felt, was his build and size. A compact and well-shaped man, by leading with his beautifully flat belly he somehow managed to highlight both attributes while in motion. A second was the quintessential masculinity of the walk. No woman could move as he did without appearing bizarre, nor did he have the neutral gait common to both sexes. In the end, however, perhaps the most agreeable feature of the way he moved was that it was so much "him." Had he put on a black wig, shaved off his beard, distorted his features, and even padded his body, a few steps would still have revealed his identity to anyone who knew him (*see* Attitudes: Health maintenance; Biography/His: Leanness; Love/General: Monogamy; and Self-image/Contributing to: Muscle).

JOINT

Ancestors: Of the two, he'd been less forthcoming about his ancestry than she. He did tell her his father's family was originally German and had arrived in England via Holland several hundred years ago;

that his mother's family was English all along and that somewhere in his background there was Jewish blood. Such scraps of information, however, were not the equivalent of colourful stories, but then she knew that in England the circumstances of one's foreign forebears (assuming they *were* foreign) did not occupy the same conversational niche as in the United States (*see* Biography/Hers: Galicia, Hungary).

Attraction (mutual): S*ee* Biography/Summary/His: various; Biography/Hers: America, Jew; Biography/Joint: Courtship; Love/Summary; and Sex/Summary.

Courtship: The pair's courtship was extremely swift. After their first date, he'd sent her a note of appreciation, and she'd rung the mutual friend who'd introduced them to ask why she hadn't done it sooner. A week later, he told her that for the first time with a woman he could relax utterly, and she began to fantasise about him as a lover. The fantasy soon became a preoccupation, since he seemed to be shy. She decided to wait three weeks (her notion of the minimum decent interval) and then proposition him outright. Though a bit staggered by her bluntness, he'd accepted (*see* Biography/Joint: Attraction [mutual]; Love: all categories; and Sex/Summary).

Election (local): S*ee* Attitudes: Politics and Biography/Joint: Meeting, first.

Empire State Building: During their time in New York, he'd expressed a desire to see the city from the top of the Empire State Building. She had hoped he'd already "done" the Empire State, as she could think of few more embarrassing activities. She'd agreed all the same—at least until they walked inside the building and she heard how much it was going to cost for the two-minute ride in the lift. She announced in a very loud voice that when she was a small child, the same ride had been free and that she'd consent to pay half, but not a penny more. No amount of argument on his part could get her to change her mind or even calm down, and they'd left in a mutual huff (*see* Love/General: Understanding and Love/Specific: Arguing).

Flatiron Building: Alongside New York's other architectural delights, she was as proud to show off the Flatiron Building to a visitor as if she'd built the thing herself. That he had seen it on previous visits did not stop him hovering around it for extended periods of time, taking photographs from every conceivable angle, enlarging the photos, and pinning up the enlargements on the walls. The one thing he never got around to doing (much to her surprise) was to draw it (*see* Art/Subjects: Cityscape).

Grandmothers: As neither he nor she had very extensive memories of grandfathers or paternal grandmothers, discussions of that generation centred on the maternal side. She'd learned that his grandmother had lived with his family for many years, that he hadn't a solitary memory of her that wasn't warm and loving, and that her death had been the single bereavement of his life. Her experience had not paralleled his. Her father had died when she was nine, and her grandmother had moved into the apartment next door to prepare meals for her and her now-working mother. The arrangement had worked well enough until one evening when she was about sixteen. The three of them were eating together as usual when her grandmother had suddenly put down her fork, looked her up and down, and then turned to her mother and said: "I don't know. I married off four ugly daughters. Why can't you marry off one pretty one?" She and her mother had moved away shortly thereafter (*see* Biography/Hers: Hungary and Love/General: Need).

Greece (Thassos): Not counting New York (which she could not think of as "foreign"), a week-long trip to Thassos had been the single foreign holiday allowed them by fate before he'd become ill. Neither had ever been to any part of Greece before, and as far as sun, scenery, and cuisine were concerned, the island had more or less lived up to what they'd been expecting. During their time there, he had sketched almost nonstop while she had read and admired the efficient way in which the package holiday system (of which they were a part) deposited stacks of pale-skinned tourists, roasted them till they were medium or well-done, and then loaded them off as the next stacks arrived. Both had been struck by the undernourished cats that accosted one at every meal and the inevitable clusters of natives who seemed to sit around all day, drinking and gossiping. After some discussion, it was decided that a sort of vacation highlight had been the priest in a nearby village who'd enthusiastically described his church in a language that wasn't Greek but still not one that either could understand, and then given them a round embossed loaf of bread. Upon their return to England, she'd taken a perverse pride in being the only American on the plane and standing in her very own passport queue (*see* Biography/Joint: New York City, Travel, and Walks).

Guggenheim: While in New York, the pair had trudged to the famous museum but been so under-impressed by the current exhibition that even the promenade down the curving walkway hadn't fully compensated. It was, therefore, gratifying when they then learned of a new downtown "Guggy," actually within walking distance of where they were staying. Though as a building the new museum did not challenge the white marvel uptown, it did contain several atypical paintings by Klee that had stopped them in their tracks. One in particular showed a small cluster of houses in a wood and glowed as if painted by an angelic hand. Wanting some sort of copy, the two had searched through postcards, prints, and book plates only to conclude that no reproduction came near to capturing the magical effect of the original. They'd agreed there and then to return to the museum sufficient times to commit the painting to heart (*see* Passions/Art: Klee, P.).

Interrupting: *See* Abilities: Communication, verbal and Love/ Specific: Talking.

Meeting, first: The couple's first official date was for lunch at a pizzeria. It was a sunny spring day and they were able to sit outside. The solitary blip in the afternoon came when she mentioned that she was canvassing for the upcoming local election and couldn't stay for too long, as she was expected to put in at least two or three hours. He'd suddenly looked uncomfortable, paused, and in a small voice asked her, "Which party?" She'd answered, "The Green Party," and he'd visibly relaxed. Much later when they were living together, he confessed that had she said "Tory," things might well have gone differently between them, though, he quickly added, he somehow thought she wouldn't (*see* Attitudes: Politics; Character: Heroism; and Biography/Joint: Courtship).

New Year's Eves: Their first New Year's Eve together was at the party of a friend. Though neither were habitual partygoers, they determined to enjoy themselves and did so until the moment when she realised the following: (a) the honour of New Year's Eve seemed to require everyone carry on into the small hours of the morning; (b) with the best will in the world, she would never last much past midnight; (c) *he* could, easily, and therefore (d) because of her, he was going to have to leave ridiculously early. In the event, they hung on until just after 12:30 (her personal best), and he didn't seem too put out—though the following year they celebrated on their own (*see* Passions/Holidays: Christmas).

New York City: They had already made arrangements for a short holiday in France when her mother rang to say that she needed to have a serious operation and could they come to New York instead and take their holiday there? They duly went. The operation was a failure, and her mother died ten days later, thus forcing them to remain for a further two months (far longer than either of *his* previous visits to the city). The period in New York proved a turning point for the couple. Being together for that long (and through such a harrowing experience) convinced them that they genuinely loved each other and could not now live apart. Likewise, it catapulted his art to a new level of excellence by inadvertently providing him both with the inspiration he'd been searching for and the time to put it to good use (*see* Art/Subjects: Cityscape; Biography/Summary/Hers: New York City; and Love/General: Proximity).

Pianos: Near to death, her mother had made the couple swear that they wouldn't sell her beloved Steinway Baby Grand. Though both knew that (a) the cost of shipping the piano to England would be prohibitive and (b) that they didn't possess a room large enough to put it in, they hardly dared refuse her. And then the Steinway representative called round to advise them on shipping and began to gaze ruefully at the keyboard. These days, he informed them, there were very strict rules regarding the export and import of ivory, and (irrespective of the fact that the contributing elephant had likely died around 1930) it might take years to actually get the piano to England. That proved the proverbial straw, and they'd flogged it there and then. Some time later, he talked her into buying a digital keyboard, though he could not get her to play it. Her guilt over the sale was too overwhelming, and she'd found herself resenting its paltry number of octaves (*see* Music/Summary/Miscellaneous: Duets, Sound production).

Restaurants: For the first year or so, going out to eat was a valued activity for the pair. But then began a period of food experimentation (mostly to help his colitis, but also because every time the two would convince themselves that this or that diet really *was*—as its originator swore—the foundation of enduring good health), and the number of suitable restaurants dwindled. That said, there were two favourite haunts that no diet ever totally obliterated from their custom. Each one happened to be near where they living at the time; each boasted a "Cordon Bleu" menu and the prices to go along with it (though they generally felt the food was worth it); and each was intimate enough to allow friendship with the proprietors (*see*

Biography/Hers: Delicatessen; Diet/Summary/Exotic: Bouillabaisse; Diet/Regimens; House/Summary; and Illness/Chronic: Colitis, ulcerative).

Rituals: Aside from use of the sewing machine, there was only one other ritual that became a fixed part of the life of the two during their time together. It involved getting up at an ungodly hour on a Saturday morning, throwing one's clothes on, driving to a gigantic supermarket, buying the week's groceries, putting them in the backseat of Mini the Moocher (always a challenge), recycling their week's worth of cans and bottles, and, finally, having a cheap but tasty breakfast in the café that adjoined the supermarket. For her, not having to struggle home carrying heavy containers was a luxury he'd always taken for granted, though he was sensitive enough to her pedestrian background to be the one to pack the bags and deposit them in their car. The ritual usually ended with a bit of house-cleaning when they got back, though this was not to be the case in their second home, as an extremely competent cleaning woman had more or less come with the place (*see* Abilities: Sewing; House/Summary; and Transport/Summary).

Sable: The sable coat left her by her mother was the culmination of forty years of upwardly-mobile-fur-purchase on the part of the latter. To the couple, it represented a number of dead (though admittedly gorgeous) animals and—along with everything else made of fur—an entirely unacceptable garment. They subsequently went to her mother's furrier to sell it—a mistake, as the latter announced she would be defiling her mother's memory if she didn't wear the coat, and anyway it was very warm. They patiently explained their principles. The furrier countered with the tale of how Rita Hayworth's daughter had begged him to use an old mink of the actress as a lining for her own coat so she could "feel her mother's warmth." It was an affecting story, and the teller nothing if not a consummate salesman. Against their better judgment, they took the coat back to England only to find they could not afford to insure it (a detail the furrier had omitted). It hung on the outside of a closet door for a while—a "must see" for guests, as much as the garden—and when finally they decided it had to go, the effort involved was herculean. Because the coat had been custom-made for her short, pear-shaped mother, only one furrier in all of England would even accept the commission, and *he* made them feel he was doing them such a favour that they were ultimately grateful for the pittance he secured (*see* Attitudes: Ecology; Biography/Joint: New York City; Garden/Summary; and Self-image/Contributing to: Dress).

Seders: True to the family tradition, she would accept an invitation to a seder if one was specifically proffered. The second time this happened they were living together. They discussed whether or not to go; he wasn't too keen but she persuaded him it would be fun, and so they attended. It was not an unqualified success. She spent the whole evening feeling like a terrific fraud, whereas he seemed to be massively unaffected by everything that was happening. On their way home, she suddenly understood that if Jewish observances meant so little to her, they were bound to mean even less to him. She vowed never to subject him to one in the future, a vow that his death subsequently rendered inapplicable (*see* Biography/Hers: Passover).

Spectacles: From their very first meeting, she'd wondered how he looked without his specs. He had a small but handsome face, and the specs hid it. When they began sleeping together, her curiosity was satisfied: He looked wonderful. To all suggestions that he investigate less conspicuous frames, he invariably replied that vanity was not a sufficient reason to indulge in the great expense that replacing all his sets of glasses would involve. In reality, though, he was hearing her more than he let on, and just about the time she'd resigned herself to seeing him "glassesless" only in bed, he suddenly decided on contact lenses. The decision surprised even his optician, who had been of the opinion that he wasn't the type. And—even allowing (because his hands were so large) that often the lenses would stick to the tip of his forefinger, and it took several tries to get them in his eyes—the brief time he wore the lenses before becoming ill was pleasing to them both. She was delighted with what she considered his "true" appearance, and he loved not having anything on his nose (*see* Self-image/Contributing to: Face).

Transport: *See* Transport: all categories.

Travel: The couple's travel *in* England was not much more extensive than their travel outside it. There were two weekend trips: one to Swanage to celebrate their first "anniversary," a second to Portsmouth in connection with a play she was contemplating, and a respectable smattering of day trips. These generally occurred on a Sunday and were limited to the gardens, stately homes, parks, museums, and wildlife parks in a twenty- or thirty-mile radius of their own residence (*see* Biography/Joint: Walks and Love/General: Anniversaries).

Voice: She felt he had a wonderful-sounding voice: It particularly delighted her to hear him on tape, and she could never understand why nothing would induce him to sing. She sang all the time—a habit of which he was unusually tolerant considering his sole comment about *her* voice was that at times it was a bit too loud (usually when she was expostulating). The dislike of each for his or her particular voice was as thorough as her dislike of her accent and was not ameliorated by their knowledge that the timbre and pitch of one's voice could not, by definition, sound to others as it did to oneself.

Voting behaviour: *See* Attitudes: Politics.

Walks: She wasn't against walking in theory. As long as the way was relatively level, she could put her entire foot down on whatever was underneath it, she didn't have to use her hands, and nothing actually hindered her forward movement, she'd happily cover impressive distances. That said, she refused to clamber, let alone climb, and feeling her feet sink in bogs, mud, or knee-high vegetation invariably made her heart sink even further. He, in comparison, could scramble anywhere, at any angle, and simply ignore obstacles. This difference in locomotive philosophies was amply demonstrated on their brief trip to Swanage, when he proposed a "stroll" along the cliffs. There was one bit where you had to climb first down and then up with hands *and* feet. He went at it as if it were so many steps; she almost died on the spot. In the end, he'd had to backtrack and, never letting go of her hands, gently lead her over. He then had to apologise—profusely—for taking her there in the first place (*see* Attitudes: Hiking; Biography/Joint: Travel; Character: Laziness; and Transport: Public).

C

*C*haracter

Summary

The very different personalities of the couple tended to mask—even to themselves—how similar in character they happened to be. Looking at the sixteen character components listed, only five (i.e., Lack of chauvinism; Diffidence; Self-effacement; Youthfulness, and Organisation) were specific to one or the other partner. All others were shared by the pair—even if not generally to the same degree or utilising like modes of expression. Indeed, much the way similar attitudes had contributed to their affection, harmony of character played a large part in the compatibility the two experienced during their time together (*see* Attitudes/Summary).

Benevolence: Both of them were fundamentally charitable. As long as he lived and she felt at peace with the world, her charity was flamboyant, extending from street beggars to registered charities. His was less showy (it did not include beggars, for instance) but probably more consistent in that she could not imagine any reason—even her death—inducing him to abandon it. She, on other hand, turned her back on everything when he died and did not see herself reversing the volte-face. Even helping friends (the one activity she was still disposed toward) was no longer automatic but, in each case, reasoned out (*see* Attitudes: Ecology; Beliefs: God; and Biography/Hers: Epilogue, Job [Bible]).

Charisma: Sheer loquacity was the beginning and end of her charisma. As well as a willingness to talk on any subject, she was the fortunate possessor of a whole store of very funny stories that, in company, she could trot out in greater quantity and faster than anyone else could trot out theirs. Even when her patter didn't endear others toward her, it could leave them with an unshakable sense of her entertainment value. By contrast, he was no social performer. One became attuned only gradually to the talent, sensitivity, kindness, and gut wisdom underlying his quiet, self-effacing manner. The realisation that these qualities had come to light without discernible effort on his part could and often did turn the discoverer into a lifelong admirer and friend (*see* Abilities: Communication, verbal; Character: Self-effacement; and Illness/ Last [His]/Experiences: Doctors).

Chauvinism, lack of: *See* Attitudes: Women.

Diffidence: His initial diffidence—his attempt to take up as little space as possible—struck her terrifically the first time she saw him and prompted her to arrange a proper meeting between them. Later on, particularly after the two had become lovers, she'd asked about its origins. He'd told her it was, in part, his share of a national debility and then mentioned reasons more personal to himself, such as his experiences as a schoolboy. Throughout their time together, she remained confident that her love and example could ultimately dissolve whatever shyness might still be clinging to him (*see* Abilities: Communication, verbal; Character: Self-effacement; Love/General: Emergence; and Self-image/Contributing to: Learning).

Heroism: Each was immensely heroic in the other's eyes. For her, his was a heroism of the self-employed craftsman; the practising, self-sufficient artist and the individual who relies on himself to produce the objects he requires. For him, hers was a heroism of a maverick who'd formulated and never flinched from a singularly peculiar worldview, and who'd recognised early on the only thing she *really* wanted to do and pursued it in the face of twenty years of little if any encouragement, and (since she knew she could have never done both properly) to the exclusion of having children. How heroic the pair appeared to the *outside* world is more difficult to ascertain (*see* Abilities: various; Attitudes/Summary: Children, Ecology; Biography/His: Crafts; and Work/Summary: various).

Humourousness: Both of them had a healthy sense of humour. When being funny, she relied on verbal repartee, whereas he loved physical clowning. Each one could always amuse the other—in fact, his antics often made her laugh out loud and wonder at the variety of accents, impersonations, and movements he seemed to have at his command. Even when they weren't the source, the pair also tended to laugh at the same things—though not invariably. Before coming to England, she had seen a sci-fi spoof called *Dark Star* and been sufficiently impressed to declare it the funniest picture ever made. When finally she'd managed to get a video copy, he'd sat and watched it from beginning to end with folded arms and an expression not unlike the one he'd worn at her mother's funeral. Even allowing the film wasn't the masterpiece she'd remembered, it wasn't *unfunny*; in fact, a few bits were still, in her opinion, little gems. She'd puzzled over his reaction and finally concluded that probably she'd praised it too highly, a sure recipe for contrariness (*see* Love/Specific: Laughter and Passions/Cinema: Cinema).

Intelligence: Early on, he'd definitively pronounced her the brighter of the two and, before she could protest, added that he always tended to attract very intelligent women. Since the second half of his statement seemed to be a compliment, she avoided telling him that at least a part of her intelligence was nothing more than a demeanour she'd perfected in her schooldays. In any case, it wasn't likely she could have convinced him that they were far more equal than he imagined. *His* schooling had left him with the twin verities of his general stupidity and inability to learn that even the subsequent acquisition of considerable artistic and professional skills had been unable to challenge (*see* Art: various; Biography/His: School; Passions/Cinema: Cinema: Self-image/Summary/Contributing to: Learning, Literacy; and Work/Summary/His: Carpentry).

Kindness: In varying degrees, each was kind to others. Her kindness tended to be acute: It could spring up in certain situations and even slop over. That notwithstanding, the recipient soon realised that it came with a set of limitations and was bound to be replaced with an active hostility if, for any reason, she thought it had been abused. By comparison, his kindness was chronic and conditionless—a living part of him much like speech or appearance. During their time together, she rarely saw him turn anyone down for anything—even if it meant extensively cutting into his own work time—or refuse those who'd taken advantage of him in the past (*see* Character: Sensitivity and Illness/Last [His]/Experiences: Doctors).

Laziness: Every so often, each would succumb to laziness. With someone as active as himself, it was usually replacing an important activity with a pointless one for as long as he possibly could, though such behaviour often involved reluctance as well as idleness. In any case, it was never the total indolence she could effect, usually as a couch potato. In areas such as chores, they probably shared more strictly in principle than in practise, though it was not unknown for her to consciously overcome a languor that in pre-*him* days would have been the norm (*see* Art/Concepts: Incubation and House/Miscellaneous: Chores).

Morality: The two, both before they met and after, had a strong sense of honour in dealing with others. All the time he'd worked as a carpenter, he'd been scrupulous as to the quality of work and the bills he then tendered. For her part, she would have never dreamed of spending beyond her means or using any reason whatever to delay or avoid payment of what she owed. As a couple, they presented a front that verged on the naive and, long past when they should have known better, continued to expect *their* standards in others. Thus did questions as to their integrity (as when they were asked by an electrician if he could actually cash the cheque they'd given him or did he have to wait) continually surprise them, no less than attempts to cheat them both disappoint and wound (*see* Abilities: Finances; Beliefs: Spirituality; Love/General: Trust; Money: Budget; and Work/His: Carpentry).

Organisation: She was the undisputed master organiser of the two. Never, during their time together, did he observe a document of hers to go astray or ever take more than forty-five seconds to locate; a house-key of hers that didn't have its assigned place, which she never forgot; or a business letter without its copy for the files. As to files, both of them understood hers were and always would be in immaculate order and up-to-date, even when—as in their original home—there'd been no specific room or cupboard for them. He'd viewed all this with silent amazement and pondered what he felt about it. Part of him considered it irritating and felt positively tender toward the semichaos in which he operated. Another part couldn't help being grateful that at least one of them didn't waste hours looking for items that were invariably under one's nose or trying to recall the contents of one's last letter to the Gas Board. Ultimately, the latter proved more irresistible, and he'd succumbed to her organisational proclivities (*see* House/Summary; Love/Summary; and Wills/Summary).

Practicality: Both of them were only too aware of the importance of any couple agreeing on what was practical to undertake as against what wasn't. It was thus a relief on both sides to discover that neither was particularly foolish about financial matters and that his status as the "doer" of the pair insured that they would be able to afford and achieve any project he envisioned. Indeed, so completely was that the modus operandi during their time together—particularly in their second home—that only his death and the illness that preceded it prevented all of his initial projects for their home and garden from being completed (*see* Abilities: various; Character: Morality; House/Challenges: various; and Money: various).

Self-effacement: In many areas, his diffidence merged into self-effacement. One such was compliments: He tended to find high praise disconcerting. While among his friends it was understood that one never hurled very much at him, she believed she could not give him enough. In her eyes excellence was next to godliness, and she couldn't help but acknowledge those who achieved it. Too, she hoped her praise might act as a corrective to all the anti-praise he'd gotten in his youth, though she would never have paid him empty compliments, as he would have seen through them. Allied to his embarrassment at praise was his inability to don the egotism required for success in one's profession. Interestingly, neither could she, though self-effacement happened to be the last thing *she* suffered from. In the event, they both promised to promote each other's work, a promise she began to keep in earnest after his death (*see* Biography/His: School; Character: Diffidence; Self-image/Summary/Contributing to: Literacy; and Work/Summary).

Sensitivity: During their time together, each one occasionally experienced an oversensitivity or annoyance at certain habits of the other. Happily, these were never suffered in silence, and the transgressor thus had the opportunity to reform—which each would do to the extent he or she could remember about it. *Positive* sensitivity, on the other hand, was not shared by the pair. While his own vulnerability gave him a virtual sixth sense in understanding the feelings of others and knowing how to respond, there'd been nothing to develop a like sense in her. To the degree sensitivity operated in her at all, it tended to focus on him alone (*see* Abilities: Communication, verbal; Character: Charisma; Love/General: Understanding; Pets: various; and Self-image/Contributing to: Dress, Neckties).

Sociability: *See* Abilities: Communication, verbal; Character: Charisma; and Illness/Last (His)/Experiences: Doctors.

Youthfulness: Until the onset of his final illness, he'd seemed wonderfully youthful, neither looking anywhere near the age he happened to be nor revealing it in his playfulness or humour. That an individual could reach his fifties with any sort of youthfulness intact was no small achievement to one who'd secretly felt middle-aged since her teens. Admittedly, there'd been a hint of the same in the boyish antics of her first love, though his unannounced rides on supermarket trolleys were both singular and rare (*see* Art/Concepts: Imagination; Biography/His: Leanness, Walk; Biography/Joint: New Year's Eves: Character: Humourousness; and Illness/Summary).

Cookery

Summary

The pair's cooking abilities were of different orders entirely. He was confident and adventurous; she'd only recently discovered the whole business could be rewarding. While the genesis of his happy condition was unknown to her, she was the product of a grandmother who'd been a culinary genius but no teacher, and a mother who'd classed meal preparation alongside toilet disinfection among her preferred activities. When the couple met, she'd created only two original dishes in her entire life, and these she'd serve up with wearisome regularity to self and guests alike. He, by contrast, had an impressive number of recipes to his credit and was known for his entertaining. Not surprisingly, she became his pupil, though as long as he was well (and irrespective of whose recipe it might be based on), both were far too democratic not to prepare the meals jointly (*see* Abilities/Summary: Baking and Biography/Hers: Passover).

PRESENTATION OF FOOD

Before meeting him, she'd never much cared about the appearance of the food she prepared. It was sufficient if it was reasonably tasty and made no one ill. Besides, the length of time it remained on the plate altogether (let alone artistically arranged) was, in her opinion, too negligible to be a consideration. Her thinking in this regard, however, considerably altered once the two began to live together. Even just for them, he was always careful about how a meal looked, while for guests he employed an artistry that was downright Japanese in its final effect. And it was appreciated: people actually commented. She soon felt an urge to do likewise, though he died too soon for her to learn more than a fraction of his methods, which anyway might have been instinctive (*see* Abilities/Summary and Art: various).

RECIPE BOOKS

Personal: He kept a personal book of recipes, clearly written out (though not always by him) and bound in a small red book. Printed recipes, whether slipped into the front of the book or the folder he'd titled *recipes* (but which actually contained as much gardening information) tended to lack the cachet of those that had been written down and were almost never referred to. Early on, he'd explained that no recipe could be inscribed before it had been tried out, which—given the amount of suspense that could involve— meant that new entries were always a sort of an occasion for the pair (*see* Abilities: Baking; Character: Organisation; Cookery/Summary; and Love/General: Pleasure).

Published: Not counting pull-outs from magazines or newspapers, he'd possessed no less than twenty-five cookery books. One of them was so old she'd wondered that next to the ingredients they hadn't also listed necessary ration points; the others mostly had to do with different sort of diets or categories of food. *Her* contribution had been a single book from her mother—an all-purpose compendium that included not only American cuisine but a generous helping of "immigrant" recipes. They'd both agreed the latter was a fairly useful reference so long as one remembered the difference in measurements and the necessity of reducing all quantities of sugar by two-thirds (*see* Cookery/Summary and Diet: various).

SPECIALTIES

HERS

Honey-orange chicken: This recipe was completely her own invention and called for mixing orange juice with heated acacia honey, pouring it over the chicken, dotting the latter with slabs of butter, baking the whole thing uncovered in a very hot oven for fifteen minutes, and then covering it and turning the oven down to hot for further baking for an hour or so, depending on size. There had been a time when bits of garlic had also been inserted under the skin of the bird, but his stomach condition had soon made this impossible and, anyway, she'd decided it had tasted better without it.

Mulled wine: This ranked as less an original than an adaptation of recipes garnered from a favourite pub and a neighbour's cookery book. It called for equal parts of red wine and water, a sprinkling of cloves, several sticks of cinnamon, a generous helping of sugar, and pieces of lemon and orange, all of which were simmered for about twenty-five minutes before serving. The latter, incidentally, was generally the downside of mulled wine, since it required a constant vigil on the part of the preparer to see the concoction didn't boil away, thus engendering (as the preparer was usually also one of the hosts) a body crush of considerable magnitude and duration in the immediate vicinity of the cooker.

Salmon loaf: She'd made this dish for so many years that by the time the couple met she was unable to recall how she'd first thought it up.

It called for 1 large and 1 medium can of red salmon, 2 onions, the juice of 1/2 lemon, 3/4 of a tumbler of sweet sherry, 2 eggs, breadcrumbs, and mixed herbs. One mashed up all the salmon, added sufficient breadcrumbs to absorb all the moisture, chopped and sautéd the 2 onions until transparent, beat the eggs, and added them along with the remaining ingredients. When everything was thoroughly combined, one put the mixture in a greased loaf tin and baked it in a hot oven for 40–45 minutes. The beauty of the loaf was that it probably tasted better cold the following day than hot when made. She remembered being in New York one winter when her mother seemed to be having it for breakfast, lunch, and dinner. She'd offered to show her mother how to make the thing herself, but all the latter would agree to was her laying in a store of six or seven loaves before her scheduled return to England (*see* Cookery/ Summary and Biography/Hers: Passover).

Vegetarian cassoulet: This was *sort* of her recipe, for although she'd been given the ingredients by someone else, they had neglected to mention quantities—which she'd had to improvise. The genesis of the cassoulet was somewhat interesting, having been created by a young man for his vegetarian mother-in-law to have while everyone else tucked into their Christmas turkey and trimmings. Apparently, the cassoulet was so delicious that, over the years, the turkey-eaters came round to having it as well. The recipe called for 1 or 2 tins of cannellini beans, 2 tins of whole peeled chestnuts, 1 large beef tomato, cut into small pieces, 1/2 lb. of mushrooms, finely chopped, 1 zucchini, chopped into pieces, 1 small tin of tomato puree, 1/4 cup of extra virgin olive oil, or more if necessary, 1 or 2 tablespoons of brown sugar, mixed herbs, and 2 bay leaves. One thoroughly mixed all the ingredients in a large bowl and then transferred them to a large covered cooking dish, which went into a medium hot oven for at least 1 hour and 30 minutes, stirring every 30 minutes or so. During their time together, the number of her strict vegetarian friends (as compared to the fish eaters) grew, and he'd always had a lot to start with. This was the only posh dish *she* knew of to give them, though the price it exacted in wind (to servers and servees alike) was high (*see* Diet/Regimens: Vegetarian).

His

Biscuits: S*ee* Abilities: Baking.

Dumplings: These were generally made from a flour, egg, and milk mixture, with a bit of salt added. At times, he would become lazy and buy a dumpling mix from the supermarket—sometimes with a suet base, sometimes not, but always with water as the only other ingredient. She tended to find most of his dumplings dense and chewy, particularly when compared to the feather-light matzo balls her grandmother used to make for special occasions. That said, since *she* could not have made a proper matzo ball to save her life, comparisons were hardly in order and she'd kept *shtum* (*see* Abilities: Baking; Character: Laziness; Cookery/Summary; and Love/General: Openness).

Mushroom pâté: As she detested mushrooms, she'd never paid much attention to how this was made, though it was standard fare for their parties. As far as she could recall, it involved chopping and sautéing a mess of mushrooms, leeks, and garlic until it was all reduced to a sort of goop, then adding cider vinegar, soy sauce; pepper, paprika, coriander, and cumin and leaving it for twenty-four hours. To her, the finished product was unspeakable-looking, resembling nothing so much as vomit. Guests invariably loved it, however (*see* Cookery/Summary and Diet/Healthful: Mushrooms).

Non-alcoholic punch: Of all of his specialties, none had intrigued her more. To either grape juice or a mix of grape, apple, and orange juices he'd add 2 ounces of hops and 2 teaspoons each of angelica, fennel, feverfew, licorice, comfrey, peppermint, dandelion, and bay and boiling water. Since the hops and some of the herbs could require tracking down, he generally kept these all year-round in a special container, thus adding to the sort of witch's brew aura that its preparation invoked. The taste was probably more startling than pleasant, though its propensity to convince the drinker that he or she was getting drunk was universal (*see* Diet/Summary/Compulsive/Harmful: Whiskey).

Pancakes: His recipe for these had been pretty standard: eggs, salt, flour, and milk—or even prepared pancake mix. What hadn't been standard, however, was his unfailing sense of the exact heat needed so as not to undercook or burn a single one, not even the first few. Even more startling—given how much he loved to eat them—was restricting pancake preparation (and consumption) to Shrove Thursday in spite of (a) his general attitude toward Christianity and (b) the number he'd had no compunction about gobbling during their time in the United States, though it had been autumn (*see* Beliefs: Religion and Biography/Joint: New York City).

Pastry: *See* Abilities: Baking.

D

*D*iet

Summary

Due primarily to his chronic stomach problems, the diet of the pair fluctuated. During their time together, four regimens were tried— each one following a not-dissimilar course of commencement, violation, and repeal. To one who—bar those foods she'd been allergic to—had generally eaten whatever took her fancy, it was an interesting way to pass the time. There seemed to be little he didn't know about healthy eating and few books he hadn't procured about this or that gastronomic route to soundness. And yet (with the exception of a teetotalism adopted in their second year), he was constitutionally unable to stick to any regimen for an extended period, or even permanently renounce things that he knew were harmful to him. Invariably, his willpower would simply melt in the vicinity of a goody, and he would proclaim: (a) "Well, just this once, since we're eating out" or (b) "Well, we're on holiday, and what's a holiday if you can't have what you want" or a variation (c) "Well, it's Christmas" (which he appeared to regard as a license to poison himself). Time and again, she'd force herself to be pleased for him as he'd dig into something he'd solemnly sworn never to touch again. After his death, she was grateful that she *hadn't* spoken up as he'd probably been past the point of being helped even before they'd met (*see* Biography/His: Leanness; Biography/Joint: Restaurants; Diet/Compulsive/Harmful: various; Illness/Chronic: Allergy, Colitis, ulcerative; and Passions/Holidays: Christmas).

Compulsive/Harmful

Bacon: His attitude toward bacon had depended on whether it was English or American. With English rashers he was able to progress from chronic consumer to one who could give it a miss nine times out of ten. Its American cousin, on the other hand, he found irresistible. During their stay in New York, he'd had it every time they'd breakfasted out (which was often), assuring her all along that he was getting the craving for it out of his system once and for all, and anyway the usual restrictions didn't apply on holiday, which this was, sort of. She hadn't found an answer to either observation. It was sufficient that American-style bacon (which, incidentally, she *also* preferred) did not seem to be on the point of making its way to their part of England (*see* Biography/Joint: New York City; Diet/Summary; and Diet/Compulsive/Harmful: Ham).

Beef: The controversy over mad cow disease came close to putting the last nail in the coffin regarding beef. Neither of them were terrific beef eaters, and even his periodic surrenders to red meat generally excluded it. During their time together, his beef consumption had been limited to the very occasional pepper steak or steak and kidney served in a posh restaurant and the rare times when his eye happened to light on packages of Scottish beef in the supermarket. In the first case due to the fancy prices and in the second to a sort of Burnsian fantasy of rugged cattle roaming the Highlands, he'd dismiss fears of mad cow disease and maintain nothing was going to happen to them. Happily, nothing had (*see* Diet/Summary and Biography/Joint: Restaurants).

Brandy: Even when he was still drinking, he'd never had a particular liking for brandy. She, on the other hand, religiously consumed her two little glasses daily and was not happy to run out. Seeing this, he'd not unnaturally concluded that (a) brandy was probably as important to her as whiskey was to him, (b) she could taste the difference between cognac, brandy, and armignac and would have a preference, and (c) this preference would likewise extend to brand names. As it happened, he was wrong on the last two counts (*see* Diet/Summary/Compulsive/Harmful: Whiskey).

Cakes/Cookies: He hadn't just had a sweet tooth—he'd had a sweet mouth. Out of his many no-nos he probably succumbed to cakes the most often. That said, it was almost always when dining out and (unless in a gourmet restaurant where all restraint was thrown to the wind) confined to simple forms: a Danish, for example, rather than a full-blown gâteau (*see* Abilities: Baking; Biography/Joint: Restaurants; Cookery/Recipe books: Published; and Diet/Summary).

Chocolate: While he would eat chocolate if it happened to be around, she was a certifiable chocoholic. Though her habit was limited to plain rather than the more common milk chocolate, that didn't necessarily save her from abuse as the former *was* available with a bit of effort. Indeed, some years before they'd met, she'd discovered a particular German chocolate biscuit that was heaven in an undersized, overpriced box. For a time, she'd believed she could take them or leave them. When she finally saw she couldn't, she'd had to convince the shop to sell her only one box per shipment, no matter the actual number she sought to buy. The whole experience had been so humiliating, she'd ultimately given up the biscuits (and then chocolate) entirely.

Coffee: Of the two, he had been less passionate about coffee. Knowing how it didn't agree with him, he'd increasingly cut it out of his diet until he was drinking no more than the occasional cappuccino—and even that was ultimately relinquished without too much grief. She, by comparison, needed coffee only slightly less than chocolate and was so fussy about taste that she would have drunk muddy water before imbibing instant. Perhaps their most interesting coffee experience was the Christmas they splurged on a fabulously expensive Jamaican blend, only to discover that neither of them could actually discern any flavour (*see* Diet/Compulsive/Harmful: Chocolate and Passions/Holidays: Christmas).

Ham: The couple's differing attitudes toward ham reflected attitudes learned in childhood. As a Christian, it had always been an accepted part of his diet, though during their time together, he had restricted his consumption to exotic varieties purchased for the weekend or such occasions as Christmas. She, by contrast (though from a Jewish-agnostic background in which bacon and Chinese ribs had been routinely consumed), had never tasted ham in her entire life or—given the choice—ever intended to. Before he had been able to point out the inconsistency in her behaviour, *she* had pointed out that it stemmed from an illogical revulsion to the stuff which she'd inherited from her mother, who'd inherited it from *her* mother, in whom it had been based on religious-cultural scruples and was therefore not illogical at all (*see* Beliefs: Religion and Passions/ Holidays: Christmas).

Jam, other spreads: The pair were fairly united in their dislike of ultrasweet spreads, though her dislike was universal while his was place-specific. In restaurants, for example, he'd insist on strawberry preserve, knowing full well that the little squares it came in undoubtedly contained more sugar than fruit. At home, by comparison, he would content himself with sugarless orange marmalade. Now and then the couple would receive gifts of jams or other spreads, which usually remained unopened in the fridge until mould set in. The one exception to this had been some heavenly apple butter that close friends had brought them from North Carolina and which they'd come near to fighting over before it finally ran out (*see* Biography/Joint: Restaurants and Diet/Summary).

Onions: Long before they'd first met, he had not been able to tolerate onions. She, in comparison, dearly loved them, though for his sake she'd promised to try and eat fewer. And then fate stepped in in the form of a diet which forbade *her* onions as well, and that was that. When she'd subsequently complained that giving up onions had rendered one of her two recipes in the whole world useless, he'd replied that she could use leeks instead. For some reason, their diets didn't prohibit them, and anyway he'd always been able to eat leeks without ill effect. So she'd switched, though not without a pang (*see* Cookery/Specialties/Hers: Salmon loaf and Diet/Regimens: Tibetan).

Pork: *See* Diet/Compulsive/Harmful: Ham.

Sausages: He'd had a passion for sausages that was a close second to his passion for American bacon, whereas she—over and above inherited cultural considerations—quite frankly found every variety (including vegetarian) revolting. So extreme was her reaction that she'd once asked him if he could think of any other junk food that looked more the *part* than a sausage. But all he'd done was bristle at the junk-food designation. And even granting that sausage consumption *chez eux* was a rare and exceptional event, in restaurants he never thought twice about scoffing as many as he could (*see* Biography/Joint: Restaurants and Diet/Compulsive/Harmful: Ham).

Sugar: Other than her taking sugar with her cappuccinos when dining out, the couple pretty much came to eliminate this particular item from their diet. Their home supply consisted of the one "allowed" sugar, namely, unrefined Jamaican Muscavado, and even this was seldom used. Indeed, when sugar-consuming guests came for tea, one of them would usually have to hack away at the block the Muscavado would have inevitably become until something akin to spoonable crystals were achieved (*see* Cookery/Recipe books: Published and Diet/Healthful: Honey, Maple syrup, Strawberries).

Tea: The pair's range of teas had, in number, rivalled his cookery books. Every one of them, bar ordinary tea, was reputed to be okay, although personally she got confused over (a) tannin vs. caffeine, (b) which particular teas had one, the other, or neither, and (c) whether fancy-flavoured varieties (such as apple cinnamon) were comparable in benefits to natural ones like camomile. *He,* by comparison, hadn't seemed to be particularly bothered and would drink ordinary or any other sort simply as the spirit moved him. Perhaps the most persistent aspect of their tea consumption was her (American) habit of refusing to take milk with it (*see* Cookery/Recipe books: Published; Diet/Compulsive/Harmful: Coffee; and Diet/Healthful: Herbal tea).

Whiskey: Prior to his successful New Year's resolution of no alcohol (because drinking made the back of his neck itch), he had dearly loved his whiskey. Before they'd met, he'd already been conditioned (through his American connections) to the happy hour and had made his own connection of the hour to the drink. During their time in New York, the couple had first adopted the hour for themselves, though for her it happened to mean brandy. Whichever, she had always made certain that it was as replete with snacks as booze in the hope that the whiskey might do him less harm if not consumed on its own. An interesting footnote regarding their intake of spirits was the marked difference in the respective palates of the two. While he could easily distinguish between different nationalities and/or qualities of whiskey, *she* could have drunk brandy-flavoured lighter fluid and been content (*see* Biography/Hers: America; Biography/Joint: New York City; and Diet/Compulsive/Harmful: Brandy).

Wine: While genuinely pleased that he had quit drinking, she had sorely missed having a glass or two of wine with dinner. When he'd then told her to go ahead and have one anyway, she had tried but had generally found that his abstention engendered a guilty miasma sufficiently powerful to render consumption of even the best wines joyless. All in all, it was a lot easier at the homes of friends or while eating out, where the presence of other drinkers appeared to convince her that she wasn't letting down the team (*see* Diet/Summary/Compulsive/Harmful: Whiskey).

Exotic

Bouillabaisse: While first having eaten bouillabaisse many years back on a trip to Marseilles, she could not actually recall the taste. What *had* stuck in her mind was (a) the contempt of the waiters when she and her companions had sat down for dinner well before what the former considered its normal hour (i.e., 9:00 P.M.), (b) the trimmed-down version served to non-Frenchmen, since (in the opinion of the locals) no foreigner could manage genuine bouillabaisse, which apparently contained every fish in the ocean, and (c) the £200 the "Anglo version" had cost for the four of them—trimmed down or not. He, by contrast, must have had his first bouillabaisse in far happier circumstances because he adored it and was thrilled to discover that the Cordon bleu chef of a nearby and much-beloved haunt liked to make it. If it was on the menu, he'd always order a bowlful, and though the bowl was about 1/16 the size of the bowls she remembered from France, it was enough to serve as his entire meal. Unfailingly, he would proclaim it as good as the real thing (though—given her own experience—how he could have ever tasted "the real thing" she didn't know) and extravagantly compliment the chef (*see* Biography/Joint: Restaurants and Passions/America: West, American).

Lychees: His patent love of tinned lychees seemed to conflict with a stubborn notion that they were sufficiently exotic to be consumed only now and then. During their time together, he'd never once bought a tin, and they weren't generally available in restaurants, apart from Chinese ones. Indeed, coming upon fresh lychees one time in a local Indian restaurant had ranked as a bit of an event for the pair. Since the word *fresh* hadn't appeared next to *lychees* on the menu, they had waited for his usual little dish of transparent white globules in transparent syrup when—lo and behold—a handful of small brown hairy things appeared inside. Unperturbed, he'd soon figured out how to extract the contents and thoughtfully munched away (*see* Biography/Joint: Restaurants).

HEALTHFUL

Cheese: Before meeting him, she had believed that all cheese (sort of by definition) was healthy. Living together, however, had soon changed that. Most cheese, he'd explained, contained too much fat to be anything like healthy—particularly, as it turned out, all the cheeses (hard *and* soft) the two of them really loved. So (both for his sake and out of a general principle), they had experimented with vegetarian and low-fat varieties only to discover (yet again) the iron law of food: The healthier the item, the lousier the taste. For once united in their recidivism, they probably would have gone on eating high-fat delights had it not been that two out of their four diets happen to absolutely ban them, and they got out of the habit (*see* Diet/Regimens: various).

Goat's milk: Practically down the road from their home in the country, there had been a supplier of goat's milk. He would buy it now and then because (a) as a goat was simpler than a cow, it meant that the milk was more easily digestible and (b) it was obviously fresher than any milk that could be had from a supermarket. She had tried it for a time but had found the taste unpleasant. While he'd told her she'd eventually get used to it, she hadn't particularly wanted to, though she had pleaded an inability to drink full-fat milk (which wasn't untrue) as the reason. He'd continued drinking the stuff for a while after that, though as he could never get through even the smallest amount before it went off, he'd likewise reverted to cows in the end (*see* Diet/Healthful: Cheese, Tofu; House/ Summary; and Pets/Summary).

Herbal tea: *See* Diet/Compulsive/Harmful: Tea.

Honey: It was impossible for one as conscious of correct eating as he was not to have long ago substituted honey for sugar, and during their time together, she hadn't been particularly surprised to see him routinely spoon different varieties into teas and onto breads. She, by contrast, had always found the taste of one and all honeys cloying, though she did use one kind in one of her two recipes in the whole world, and very occasionally dipped into the honey of the moment on those mornings she condescended to a piece of toast (*see* Cookery/Recipe books: Published; Cookery/Specialties Hers: Honey-orange chicken; and Diet/Summary/Compulsive/Harmful: Sugar).

Kale: Prior to coming to England, she had never in her life seen or even heard of kale. He, on the other hand, must have been a kale eater from way back, convinced as he was of its possession of virtually every vitamin and mineral that counted and its ability to prevent cancer. In any case, they had consumed it on a sufficiently regular basis for her to reach (though not share) the following conclusions: (a) it tasted as unpleasant as it looked, (b) she didn't feel particularly healthier nor— by any other means—could she detect an increase in her mineral and vitamin level, and (c) it hadn't saved *him* from cancer (*see* Garden/Contents: Kale; Illness/Summary/Last [His]/Experiences: various; and Love/General: Openness).

Maple syrup: Under their policy of no refined sugar, he'd used maple syrup pretty much like honey, though more universally. An invariable pudding for him, for example, might be tinned pears in pear juice topped with Greek yoghurt, then topped with maple syrup. By contrast, her conception of maple syrup had always been limited to pouring conservative trickles over pancakes and waffles and a vague notion that anything *that* sweet had to be artificial. She was, therefore, not a little surprised to learn how many uses it could have and that he'd discovered a brand sufficiently natural as to have apparently flowed directly from the maple tree into the bottle sitting in their larder (*see* Diet/Healthful: Honey, Yoghurt).

Mushrooms: On their second date, he'd invited her to his home for a meal and prepared what was obviously one of his specialties: trout stuffed with mushrooms. Not wishing to offend him, she'd eaten the mushrooms without so much as a murmur. It was probably— with the exception of her vegetarian cassoulet and the paté that was such a hit with their guests—the first and last home preparation of mushrooms during their time together. Very shortly thereafter, he had recognised that his mushroom consumption was fated to be confined to other premises (*see* Cookery/Specialties/His/Hers: various).

Oatmeal: Overall, she was not a breakfast-cereal eater. In her earlier years, various declarations about the cereal boxes containing more nutritional value than their contents had soured her to most varieties, hot and cold alike. The single exception to this rule, for some reason, was oatmeal. She would regularly pass through oatmeal cycles of several months' duration, having it daily and minding neither the boredom of its preparation nor the bother of scrubbing the pot afterward. During their time together, several such cycles occurred, and (to her delight) he'd usually join her. That said, it must be admitted that neither one could tolerate the stuff on its own: both absolutely required milk and some sort of sweetener— in his case, maple syrup and in hers, raisins (*see* Diet/Healthful: Maple syrup).

Pasta: Even as ignorant an eater as herself had heard about all the happy Italians who would never get heart disease because they ate pasta in such prodigious quantity and how the declared healthiest diet in the world (i.e., traditional Japanese) contained a large measure of it. Since, personally, she could have existed on pasta and nothing else, it was a blow when he told her that (as with cheese), life wasn't so simple. Apparently, the white pasta she relied on was, if not actually harmful, a long ways behind the soba that the cognoscenti knew to be the epitome of correct noodle consumption. Indeed, more than once he'd sought to get her to change over, but for some reason, she'd found the colour of soba utterly off-putting and had not been able to bring herself to try it (*see* Diet/Healthful: Cheese).

Potatoes: He'd adored potatoes. After they began to live together, she seemed to spend an inordinate number of hours peeling and cutting them—usually with three times the effort it took him. Potatoes had been her nemesis when very young: As a disgustingly obese toddler, the doctor had reduced her baked potato intake from one a day to one a week. Too young to understand what was going on, she'd cried bitterly but had quickly slimmed down to manageable proportions and thereafter harboured a vague prejudice against them. It was only in meeting him that she'd seen her old potato passion incarnated in a grown man and until—ironically—the Tibetan diet entirely forbade her from having them, again began to eat them not only baked with milk and butter, but in every other conceivable form (*see* Diet/Regimens: Tibetan).

Rice: Living with him, she acquired a knowledge of rice second only to that of art materials. This ranging over the entire rice spectrum came less from the search for the best taste than for the one most amenable to his digestion. He'd begun with brown rice, assuring her that it was healthier to eat than its bleached white brother. Regimen after regimen, however, soon forbade him the former, and he was back to the bleached white brother, like it or not. Then, even *that* became a no-no and he was reduced to flaked rice, which reminded her of gruel. Every variety he plowed through (from brown to basmati to wild to flaked) she dutifully bought but refused to consume, as *her* preferred rice was, sadly, the lowest of the low: white, quick-cooking, and fluffy-grained (*see* Art/Materials: various and Diet/Regimens: various).

Roe: Roe was very much his baby, so to speak. Having seen the look on her face the first time he'd bought it, he'd never once even offered her a taste. On the contrary, they'd both understood that it was bought for him alone and that its purchase inevitably presaged one of those rare evenings of every man cooking for himself. Fair enough. Seeing the look on *his* face when he had the roe, she'd somehow known better than to ask him how on earth he had come to love something so consummately unappetising. Indeed, it could be said that perhaps no other food in the couple's experience engendered a greater atmosphere of tolerance on her part (*see* Love/General: Understanding).

Rye bread: Aside from his attempts at homemade and commercial wholemeals (whose consistencies—in her opinion—could have worn down the teeth of a moose), the only bread to grace the inside of their home before his final illness was her beloved rye. Its limited availability and correspondingly astronomical price made it something of a rarity, and anyway it wasn't much like the rye of her girlhood. In the end, though, it was better than no rye at all and (when fresh) good enough to eat on its own. He, who could not conceive of bread without something on it, had marvelled every time he saw her wolf down virgin slices though no more than *she'd* marvelled at the spectacle of him toasting and then suffocating several pieces under butter and honey (*see* Abilities: Baking; Diet/Harmful: Honey; and Love/General: Understanding).

Safflower oil: For some reason, which he assumed she knew and thus never bothered to explain, safflower seemed to be *the* politically correct oil for healthy eaters. A supply was, therefore, always kept on hand, though often (and as inexplicably) he would sauté various items in butter, and both of them used olive oil to give a kick to the taste of whatever was being prepared (*see* Diet/Healthful: Scallops).

Salt: He was one of the legions who automatically put salt on their food prior to eating it. She, by contrast—particularly as her mother had not even kept salt in her home for the last fifteen years of her life—did at least first taste what was in front of her before reaching for the cellar. This difference in salt philosophy in the pair was likewise reflected in their cooking—he being a lot more heavy-handed in its use and vocal if a dish was undersalted. It was at such times that she had to remind him that *her* salt mistakes were, by definition, correctable (*see* Love/General: Understanding).

Scallops: Scallops were always a treat for the pair—particularly once they had discovered a variety of small scallops that didn't cost the earth. While fish (shelled or otherwise) had always occupied the same place in her mind as cheese as more or less healthy (polluted waterways have rendered certainty on that score a thing of the past), now and then she had wondered if his frying the scallops in garlic and butter didn't somehow lessen their virtue to a point of nullity. They were so delicious prepared this way, however, she soon worked out a little formula to alleviate her doubts: The garlic (healthful) cancelled out the butter (harmful), whereas the rice they always had with the scallops tipped the scales in favour of guiltless consumption (*see* Diet/Healthful: Cheese, Safflower oil).

Shark: His introducing her to shark as something one could *eat* and not merely fear had been a genuine surprise in her culinary experience. The sight of it—minus its teeth and ferocious temperament and cut down to harmless steaks—was no less intriguing than the realisation that if properly prepared, its taste equalled (if not surpassed) that of swordfish or bass. His own shark recipe involved soaking each steak in some kind of marinade for as many hours as possible and then baking the lot. He (and she, very early in their life together) traditionally thought enough of shark as a dish for it to be on their guest menu, even though its availability (when compared to more common fish) could never be taken for granted (*see* Diet/Healthful: Swordfish).

Shrimp: While both of them enjoyed shrimp, it never once occurred to either to buy it raw to prepare as a main course. Instead, the two invariably honed in on the precooked variety, though here they did part ways somewhat. Specifically, he was an aficionado of the unshelled while *she* felt that (a) seeing them in a state of nature was a bit too much of a reminder of what being a carnivore was all about and (b) eating lost a lot of its zest when it came down to a struggle between one and one's food. That said, he did eventually bring her round and, after a mere six attempts, even taught her how to extract the edible bits from everything else (*see* Passions/Japan: Sushi).

Skimmed milk: *See* Diet/Healthful: Goat's milk.

Strawberries: Strawberries could be tricky in the health stakes. While acceptable enough when fresh, they tended not to be very sweet, which meant either concentrating on the strawberry flavour and not minding or being obliged to cut the sourness with sugar. Indeed, the pair's strawberry consumption often came down to chipping off a few crystals from the muscavado block and being embarrassed that for once maple syrup or honey wouldn't do (him) or not particularly enjoying what was in one's mouth (her). A happy solution, however, was ultimately hit upon when the two decided to mix the strawberries together with such guaranteed sweeties as ripe bananas, peaches, and apricots into a sort of fruity goop (*see* Diet/Compulsive/Harmful: Sugar and Diet/Healthful: Honey, Maple Syrup).

Swordfish: She had eaten and enjoyed swordfish before she'd ever known him. He, on the other hand, having always known about shark as well as swordfish, had come to treat the two as one: to be purchased only in the form of steaks and prepared in an identical manner. Again unlike her, he'd also known that shark was the tastier (if less available) fish (*see* Diet/Healthful: Shark).

Tofu: Tofu occupied a near unique place in the diet of the pair during their time together. Aside from a few bizarre vegetarian equivalents of junk food, probably no other comestible was purchased as often and never used. The problem was that while its credentials as a health food were unimpeachable, its actual contribution to cuisine seemed to elude anyone who wasn't Oriental or didn't want to make the effort. Since it was he who generally insisted on buying it, she never could understand why he then would absolutely forget he had it until it was too late. Not being particularly keen on it herself, she'd never remember, either with the result that the number of untouched tofu blocks that were thrown out because they'd passed their sell-by date far outnumbered their equivalent in sour goat's milk (*see* Diet/Healthful: Goat's milk and Diet/Compulsive/Harmful: Sausages).

Whitebait: If there was absolutely no roe available, he would settle for whitebait. For her part, she'd seen and eaten whitebait before having met him, though only once—which had been enough. Thus, while it was understood that (like roe) whitebait was for him alone, the couple also knew that *unlike* the former, she could actually bear to look at the little fishes before and after they'd been prepared. A corollary of the latter was that whitebait therefore probably did not put her tolerance to quite the test (*see* Diet/Healthful: Roe and Love/General: Understanding).

Yoghurt: The yoghurt they both adored and stuck to devotedly throughout their entire time together was far from being correct, as it was full-fat and not particularly alive as far as one could tell. It was, however, thick and delicious and Greek, and nothing would have made either of them ever give it up (*see* Diet/Healthful: Cheese, Maple syrup, Skimmed milk.

REGIMENS

Hay Diet: This had involved not eating carbohydrates (starches and sugar) with proteins and acid fruits in the same meal and having to wait for at least four hours between having one and the other. All food and drink was divided into carbohydrates; proteins/acid fruits; or neutral, which (thank heaven) one could have with either the former or the latter. That notwithstanding, the two of them found the Hay a fiendish diet to follow with any rigour. As it was virtually impossible to remember what came under what category, great lists were constantly needed on kitchen walls or one's person. Rarely could either one approach even a snack without extensive reference and calculation, and to cap it all, the menus were invariably boring, since (in an interesting extension of the iron law of food) mixing carbohydrates with proteins or acid fruits seemed to be the very thing that gave food its zip. In the end, it was all too much, and with their *own* mix of disappointment and relief, the pair had thrown in the towel (*see* Diet/Summary/Healthful: Cheese).

Organic: As with vegetarianism, eating organically was less a formal diet for the two than a sort of mutual pledge to use the healthiest ingredients for everything they prepared. In their first home, where *he* had grown all their vegetables, and organic chicken and meat were available from neighbouring farmshops, it had been less of a preoccupation than in their second, where neither was so easily available. Indeed, suddenly forced to rely on supermarkets, which could be very erratic as to their stocks of organic food, the two finally came to think of the whole idea as useful rather than compulsory (*see* Diet/Regimens: Vegetarian and House/Summary).

Tibetan: On the advice of a friend who'd recommended her warmly, he'd begun to see a Tibetan doctor for his stomach problems. She'd also gone along, ostensibly for her hay fever but mostly as a gesture of support. The doctor would supply them with the appropriate Tibetan herbs for their ailments and then outline what they could and couldn't eat. As the ailments differed, quite naturally the herbs and diets did as well, and for the first time the pair was faced with routinely preparing separate courses, if not entire meals. That said, they probably stuck to their respective Tibetan diets more tenaciously than any other, since the benefits gained from so doing—though, ironically, for her rather than him—were immediate and startling (*see* Diet/Summary; Illness/Chronic: Allergy,

Colitis, ulcerative; Illness/Last [His]/Experiences: Diagnoses; and Illness/Reactions, Strategies, alternative).

Vegetarian: When he'd sat her down and solemnly announced that from that day forward, they were going to be vegetarians, she hadn't batted an eye. When he'd next begun to flip through innumerable books on vegetarian cookery, she'd contemplated her nails. But when he'd actually drawn up a day-by-day menu, she'd begun to pay attention. Perhaps he really meant it. Ultimately, she came to understand that even if he had, the impossibility of controlling their food supply would have doomed such an enterprise from the start. By then they'd lived together long enough for her to realise that merely being in the *vicinity* of a goody was sufficient for him to succumb. Indeed, unlike the organic regime, wherein the unavailability of what they wanted ultimately did in their resolve, here it was a simple failure of his will. Or so she liked to think. The truth was she wasn't a dedicated vegetarian, either. Like any other Jew with at least one competent cook in their history, she could not *really* contemplate a totally meatless existence (*see* Cookery/Summary, Diet/Summary/Compulsive/Harmful: Beef, Cakes and Cookies; and Diet/Healthful: Organic).

G

Garden

Summary

Gardening had the intriguing distinction of being at the same time a passion and a sealed book for the pair. He'd been raised on several acres of land; she—at least prior to coming to England—had been a chronic apartment dweller. He could pretty much grow whatever he set his mind to; she didn't even know that unlike leaves, grass didn't disappear in the winter. When they first met, she was renting a house with a "handkerchief garden" in back and employing a gardener for its upkeep. He, by contrast, personally tended almost a third of an acre behind his house and a fair-sized whack in front. The latter he had turned into a wonder of climbing roses, flowerbeds, hedges, trees, and a bower, while in the vastness out back he'd created more bowers; orchards; more flower beds; a tepee; a pond; enough vegetable beds to allow him near self-sufficiency at certain times of the year; a lawn to loll upon; and numerous greenhouses and potting sheds. She'd been quite stunned on first seeing it, a reaction that was surpassed upon learning the amount of work required to keep the wonder going. Indeed, even he'd expressed dissatisfaction at having to devote so much time to the garden instead of his art, and it was one of the reasons they'd subsequently moved into the city. Prior to the move, however, she'd lived with him in the country and partly because they'd sort of become *her* gardens, too, but mostly because her conscience would have never allowed him to slave away on his own (and he'd sworn it was good exercise), she'd had her first-ever meeting with the earth.

This had involved digging it, cutting back shrubs, and pulling out or cutting weeds. Looking back, she supposed she must have helped a bit—her intentions were so earnest and his compliments so unstinting—but frankly, the single thing that stood out in her mind vis-à-vis Garden No. 1 was his patient, unending explanations about which were the flowers and which the weeds. After numerous instances of sweating away for what felt like hours (but in reality were mere dollops of time), she'd finally had to conclude that her only real strengths were digging up plots where everything had to go and choosing items from the garden centre. The latter talent, incidentally, came into full flower when they acquired their second, much smaller garden in the city. After an initial bash of planning, digging, and buying most of the flora to fill it, they'd only been able to plant a few rows of vegetables before he died. After his death, she'd immediately reverted to her original behaviour and once again hired a gardener (*see* Abilities: various; Attitudes: Ecology; Biography/His: England; Biography/Hers: New York City; Character: Heroism; House/Summary; and Love/General: Understanding).

AREAS

Bowers: He'd constructed three bowers in all: a modest one in the front garden with something growing on it that wasn't roses and two out back that included little seats on either side and undoubtedly roses. As far as she could gather without having asked him, the two back bowers were intended to indicate a path of sorts for the garden wanderer, whereas the front one just stood there, looking pretty and blowing apart in every fierce wind. Once they'd moved, he'd spoken of constructing quite an involved version for the pathway of their new garden—something verging on the extended grape bowers they'd dined beneath in Greece—but sadly, death had prevented him from fulfilling the project (*see* Biography/Joint: Greece [Thassos]; Character: Practicality; and House/Summary/Garden).

Flowers: In her eyes, the variety of flowers and flowering shrubs and trees when both their gardens were taken together had been little short of magnificent. But then, she wasn't a gardener. He, however, was, and modest with it. To such a man, the grounds of parks and stately homes might be fit subjects of admiration, but hardly his own efforts. An interesting aspect of the pair's association with flowers was their respective powers of recognition. Before meeting him, her ignorance in this respect had been near all-encompassing; during their time together, she'd learned to recognise perhaps three percent of what was around. He, on the other hand, did not seem to be as knowledgeable as one would have expected of a man of the soil. Time and again, she'd ask him the name of this or that flower only to be told he hadn't the faintest idea and that she should check the little identifying label he'd planted with it. The labels, however, tended to be as fragile as his memory and would either have disappeared completely or, if still extant, faded into illegibility (*see* Abilities/Summary and Biography/Joint: Travel).

Fruit trees: The many fruit trees attached to their house in the country had all been apple, though she'd never known exactly what kind. Her memories of actually consuming the fruit were also vague: For some reason, he (as the apple enthusiast of the household) had preferred organic apples from the supermarket or farmshop to the organic ones on hand. In their second home, they'd had a single Cox apple and a single Victoria plum tree, and the second autumn she was there (he had already died), both produced a record amount of fruit. Predictably, the apples hadn't thrilled her much, but plums were a great favourite and this particular variety so uniformly delicious that she had felt a sort of duty to keep up with the tree as it produced them. Since she was too much her mother's daughter to consider preserving the plums, this had entailed (a) eating an average of twenty to thirty a day for several weeks; (b) a parallel dose of diarrhoea, and (c) ultimate failure, as she'd *still* been obliged to give away close to 150, while leaving almost as many damaged ones for the birds (*see* Cookery/Summary and Garden/Contents: Corkscrew hazel, Holly, Weeping willow).

Herbs: He'd grown such an impressive variety of herbs in their first house that she'd never bothered to learn what they all were, never mind *where* they were. Thus herb harvesting remained his thing, though preparing them for use soon became hers—a task she didn't thank him for as she never knew how each was supposed to be chopped or whether one did or didn't include the stalk. All in all, it was a lot simpler (and, in her opinion, no less tasty) to buy them dried and pour them out of a bottle or box. In their second home, he'd died before he'd had time to plant any in quantity, and (left to her own devices) she'd rarely visited the one naturally occurring thyme near their back shed (*see* Cookery/Summary; Garden/Contents: Thyme, creeping; and House/Summary).

Lawn: In their first home, the lawn area had been given over to tables and chairs rather than games like croquet. Indeed, during the milder months (if the wind was in the right direction and the smell from the nearby pig farm didn't force one indoors), it was often the location of evening drinks (when the pair was on their own) or downright food (if they were entertaining). To her, maintaining this little patch seemed a thankless business. The grass never looked healthy; mowing it was a pain, as it was bordered by several trees that grew so low one had to be horizontal to make an impression, and anyway, moles seemed to use it as much as they. In their second, much smaller garden, it was mostly grass, and they'd had enough time before he became ill to stake about one fourth specifically as a lawn for the same uses as above (*see* Garden/Inhabitants: Moles; House/Summary/Adventures: Sale).

Pond: In their first home, he'd created a wonderful pond with waterlilies, contented goldfish, and even a few frogs. While visitors always praised it, he'd never come out and say how proud of the pond he was. It was not for nothing, however, that (a) he was scrupulous about preventing it from becoming clogged with algae or whatever it was that ponds got clogged with; (b) he was always certain to top it up when there'd been a dry spell; and (c) the very first thing he did in their second garden was to dig a small, kidney-shaped hole for Pond, Mark II and then plant a miniature weeping willow just beside it (*see* Garden/Summary/Contents: Waterlilies, Weeping willow and Garden/Inhabitants: Frogs, Goldfish).

Shrubs: After only a year of them hitting her in the face and getting underfoot as she would desperately try to avoid treading on their droopy bits while bringing in the groceries, she could say with confidence that she knew a shrub when she met one. She could also say that while she'd initially thought that trimming them back would be her revenge, she'd quickly learned otherwise. Either she was faced with branches that would not yield before she'd wrenched every muscle in her back or neighbouring branches threatened her eyesight by snapping back or, after only minutes, she was covered head to toe in fluff. If she hadn't known that flora was incapable of human malice, she would have sworn that the blighters were getting their licks in first. That said, she'd had to admit that every single example around their country home warmed her heart when it was in bloom and that she was as disappointed as he when any transplanted to their city garden didn't survive (*see* Garden/Summary/Contents: various).

Vegetables: *See* Attitudes: Ecology; Character: Heroism; Diet/Regimens: Organic; and Garden/Summary/Contents: various.

Wildlife: He had strongly believed that one part of any garden should be set aside for wildlife, which meant (a) leaving it uncultivated, (b) deliberately including flora that attracted it, and/or (c) creating creature-friendly items such as birdhouses or birdbaths. While she'd seen videos of a magnificent birdhouse some twenty or thirty feet high he'd once built, it was not there when she'd moved in with him in the country. Still, he had lived up to the other parts of the ethic. Not only was all the grass in the orchard (bar a single path) left uncut, but there'd been abundant buddleia to attract butterflies. So too, in their second garden, where the grass in the area just in front of their back shed was left uncut, and buddleia had been included on the list of shrubs to purchase (*see* Garden/Contents: Buddleia; Garden/Inhabitants: various; and Pets/Summary).

Contents

Apples: *See* Garden/Areas: Fruit trees.

Asparagus: Many years ago, asparagus had passed out of her price range. Imagine, then, her surprise to discover that he actually grew it. It was interesting to see what it looked like before it turned into the stalks she knew and loved, and sheer heaven to eat. Had she actually had a chance before he'd got sick (and assuming the soil had been suitable), she'd most certainly have insisted on it in their second garden.

Berberis: While she couldn't actually recall seeing any berberis in their country garden, its handsome foliage—particularly in autumn—had sufficiently attracted their attention during endless wanders through garden centres for the pair to buy and plant one for the border of their back garden in the city. After his death, she'd decided to put several plants in the two enormous tubs out front. Again wandering through a garden centre—though this time with the gardener she now employed—she instinctively went back to it, only to remember after it was already planted that she had one out back. The gardener told her it didn't hurt to have several if she

really liked them, which, obviously, she did (*see* Garden/Summary/
Contents: Camellias).

Bluebells: She'd never thought of bluebells as something one
cultivated. Rather, they seemed to be naturally occurring like
rhubarb or their fellow harbinger of spring, snowdrops. She'd
remembered seeing bluebells now and again in their country garden
but had never asked about them, so certain in her mind was she that
they'd been none of his doing. It was therefore something of a small
shock when he'd included them on his list of items to be purchased
for their second garden—though she'd kept it to herself (*see*
Garden/Contents: various and Love/General: Openness).

Brussels sprouts: During their time in the country, brussels sprouts
had not been among the more impressive of his vegetables. While
abundant in number, they tended to remain pathetically small,
looking—at least to her—uncannily like carbuncles. He'd assured
her that while in prior years his sprouts generally surpassed the
supermarket varieties, lately, this hadn't been the case. Since at
the time of this admission they had already decided to move into the
city, he'd added that there was no point in replacing the plants,
which ordinarily would have been the answer. So, they'd eaten what
was there, but with little joy.

Buddleia: He'd had masses of buddleia in their garden in the country
for the purpose of attracting butterflies, though frankly the main
beneficiaries seemed to be cabbage moths rather than the former. So
be it. The principle was the thing, and he fully intended to carry it
over into their second city garden. Since in her opinion the vivid
purple blossoms of the buddleia were pretty attractive to humans as
well, she hadn't quibbled (*see* Garden/Areas: Wildlife).

Cabbage: Her memories of cabbage were vague. He loved cabbage
and she was certain he'd grown more than one variety—perhaps a
red kind and a white kind. When she tried to picture their actual
appearance, however, all she came up with were large, scraggly balls,
invariably chewed on by flea beetles (which frankly was just as well

since cabbage was the last thing he needed for his digestion). Interestingly, beetle destruction had not stopped him from bringing generous quantities of the stuff to the friend who'd introduced them (*see* Biography/Joint: Courtship; Diet/ Summary; Garden/Contents: Marigolds; and Illness/Chronic: Colitis, ulcerative).

Camellias: Her ultimate connection with camellias was virtually identical to that of berberis, the single difference being that when he was alive, it had not managed to attract the attention of either of the pair. Indeed, it was only after his death and at the suggestion of her gardener that she had bought it as a sister plant to the berberis (*see* Garden/Contents: Berberis).

Camomile: Convinced that camomile had one purpose only—and it wasn't to plant in between blocks of cement—her surprise approached asparagus/bluebell level when he went ahead and did just that in their second garden. Indeed, she subsequently remembered a television serial called *The Camomile Lawn* and smiled to think how she'd dismissed the title as artsy and signifying nothing (*see* Diet/Compulsive/Harmful: Tea).

Carrots: Though never approaching the rather obscene size one took for granted with commercially grown carrots, she couldn't deny that his organic variety had a far superior taste, even to organic ones on sale. She'd gratefully consumed every one as long as their supply had lasted and had made certain that they were among the few vegetables they'd manage to plant in their second garden, even though he was ill. That the city batch ultimately never equalled its country forebear was due to both his death and her subsequent brief inability even to enter the garden, let alone tend what was growing (*see* Garden/Summary/Contents: Lettuce, Radishes, Spinach).

Ceanothus: To her eyes, *ceanothus dentatus* in flower was probably one of the loveliest colours in all nature: a soft cornflower blue verging on lavender. On their trips into town from their country house, they'd often pass a glorious example of it, and she'd comment every time. He hadn't known what it was called, but happily they'd gone by another example in a public garden with someone who did, and *ceanothus* became the first garden term more complicated than *rose* that she ever thought important enough to remember. Finding the special colour wasn't hard once one knew the generic name, and for their second garden, they'd bought a bush and managed to plant it the first month or two after they'd moved (*see* Garden/Summary).

Chives: *See* Garden/Areas: Herbs.

Chrysanthemums: He'd had several different kinds of chrysanthemums in the flower beds out back: gorgeous fat pompons in reds and pinks, as she recalled. He'd never do much to them, other than have her weed around them. If it had been up to her, she would have also thinned the flowers themselves, as their own weight seemed to do them in ultimately. She never mentioned this to him, however, knowing full well that random observations from a non-gardener were scarcely helpful and anyway not what he expected.

Clematis: He'd grown clematis extensively in their first garden, and there seemed to be a reasonable amount in their second when they arrived. He, however, was of the opinion that, like a good thing in general, you could never have too much clematis, and had promptly purchased and planted even more, as a covering for the walls at the back of their house. Along with cabbage, cuttings of clematis had been the single other flora he'd given (by way of thanks) to the friend who'd introduced them (*see* Biography/Joint: Courtship and Garden/Contents: Cabbage).

Corkscrew hazel: The trees in their country garden had been too numerous to identify. In their second garden, there were a more modest number: one apple, one plum, a glorious eucalyptus, and a tree that had been grafted onto something else and that neither could identify. Smaller garden size notwithstanding, in his mind four trees were hardly excessive, and in the post-move garden splurge they'd immediately gone out and bought others. The absolute peach of the bunch (so to speak) and—next to the little ceanothus—*the* dearly beloved flora of the pair was a miniature corkscrew hazel. Its branches and trunk twisted with consummate grace; it was a marvel of a tree and its indifferent leaves didn't hang on very long. They'd planted it in his largest and most beautiful ceramic pot, where it seemed to adjust without too much trauma (*see* Garden/Areas: Fruit trees; Garden/Contents: Cypress, Holly).

Crocuses: Crocuses had stuck their heads up here and there in their first garden, and he had been keen to have them again in Garden No. 2. Thus, along with tulips and daffodils and what she'd come to group together as "immediate musts," he'd planted them just after they'd moved, and—returning the compliment—they'd appeared before he was too ill to appreciate them (*see* Garden/Contents: Ceanothus, Daffodils, etc.)

Cypress: *See* Garden/Contents: Corkscrew hazel.

Daffodils: Even *she* had loved daffodils before meeting him and had seen to it there were a few rows' worth in her handkerchief garden. After she'd begun living with him, it was of course taken for granted that different varieties would be represented wherever they were, and so they had been—only not in the way she'd expected. Instead of rows (which she'd thought were the only way daffodils *could* grow) he'd plant a flower or two or a small cluster at various points throughout the garden so that one could not look in any direction without their cheery heads nodding back. Since these daffs were often far from the flower beds proper, he would always mark them out with a small stick or bamboo cane to prevent them being accidentally trodden on when they weren't flowering. There hadn't been sufficient room in their second garden to spot them around like that, and—in a curious cycle—they'd ended up back in rows (*see* Garden/Contents: Crocuses, various).

Endive: Like kale, endive had been totally alien to her before she'd arrived in England. Even after several years as an expatriate, she'd gotten no further than imagining it a kind of lettuce and thus not something she'd buy, as she wasn't particularly fond of the latter. All that changed, however, when she'd met him and they'd begun living together, since—like asparagus—he happened to grow it. She'd quickly learned it wasn't lettuce but a salad plant in its own right, with a very distinctive flavour. Though they hadn't thought to plant it in their city garden, she had assumed that at some point he would have got round to so doing (*see* Diet/Healthful: Kale and Garden/ Contents: Kale, Lettuce).

Feverfew: *See* Garden/Areas: Herbs.

Hebe: One of the flowering shrubs purchased when the couple had acquired their little set of new trees for the city, it, too, had been transferred into one of his wonderful ceramic pots, though not the supremely beautiful one set aside for the corkscrew hazel. Perhaps it had resented getting second best; perhaps it had sensed his death or (more likely) simply hadn't liked being transplanted, but slowly and systematically it seemed to be dying. Not really able to stand the death of any living thing after watching *him* die, it was only when the new gardener told her that sometimes flora that looked dead had a surprising way of reviving the following spring that she'd postponed being upset (*see* Biography/Hers: Epilogue; Garden/Contents: Corkscrew hazel; and Illness/Last [His]/Experiences: Nursing home).

Holly: This was the third of the trees the couple bought and transplanted into ceramic pots for their city garden. While not unusual as a species, the particular kind they'd chosen—a wonderful blue-green variety—perhaps was less well known. As far as she was concerned, this "Blue Angel" holly was a perfect complement to the ceanothus, which she'd convinced him was the centrepiece of the garden and the flora all others had to match. In any case, the holly had lived up to its tough leaves and was thriving (*see* Garden/Contents: Ceanothus, Cypress).

Hyacinths: Like chrysanthemums, hyacinths had been a prominent feature of their first garden in the country. They'd certainly intended on having them in Garden No. 2 and had bought a wonderful Blue

Giant variety, but she could not recall whether any had been planted immediately after they'd moved. Probably not, as other bulbs or bulbous plants had come up in time for him to see, even though he was already ill. Since they'd chosen that particular variety because its colour complemented that of the ceanothus, she fully intended to have the gardener put them in the following autumn (*see* Garden/Summary/Contents: Ceanothus, Crocuses, Holly).

Hydrangeas: Along with the rest of the flora bought and planted just after the move, the couple purchased a hydrangea as one of several climbers to hide the deplorable cladding on the front of their new home. A bit irrationally, she'd somehow expected that with so many different varieties, the cladding would immediately be covered, and was not a little disappointed when she discovered how pathetically small the climbers happened to be (*see* Garden/Contents: Pyracantha, Virginia creeper).

Irises: As both of them (in their own fashion) had grown irises prior to their time together, it was hard for her to subsequently understand why neither had included them on the planning lists for Garden No. 2. Their mutual pleasure in the flower was self-evident, and the species came in sufficient colours to have found at least one that wouldn't have clashed with the ceanothus. Quite likely, the oversight had occurred from something as inconsequential as having made all their choices before reaching "I" in the gardening encyclopedia and/or garden centres (*see* Garden/Contents: Ceanothus, Hyacinths).

Kale: To a kale enthusiast such as himself, it was inevitable that he'd be a grower rather than rely on shops for his supply. Certainly, had it not been so abundant in their country garden, she would have never eaten the stuff in such quantity (and been able to form her own less generous opinion) (*see* Diet/Healthful: Kale and Garden/Contents: Endive).

Leeks: While she couldn't remember if there had been any in the country garden, ultimately having to use leeks instead of onions in their diet had convinced him it was worth planting them in the city. He'd duly purchased seeds, but as it had been the wrong time of year to put them in along with the lettuces, carrots, and spinach, they were never sowed before he died (*see* Diet/ Compulsive/Harmful: Onions; Garden/Contents: Lettuce, Carrots, Spinach).

Lettuce: He'd loved lettuce and had had respectable amounts of several varieties in their country garden. So, too, in the city—like carrots (and some varieties of spinach), it had been one of the few vegetables she had planted under his supervision when he was already ill. Unlike the carrots, however (and ironically since *she* didn't particularly like it), the three varieties in their city garden had done so brilliantly that after his death she'd been obliged to give most of it away (*see* Garden/Contents: Carrots, Endive, Leeks, Radishes, Spinach).

Lupins: Lupins had been a distinctive and glorious feature of his garden in the country. While they had bought seeds for a handsome variety called Russell Strain, his last illness had robbed them of the chance even to open the package. Since cultivating lupins, however, apparently involved a lot more work than just planting the seeds in the ground and waiting for nature to kick in, at some point she planned to ask her new gardener if, in her opinion, it was worth it to go through the former.

Marigolds: Of all the flora she was introduced to during their time in the country, marigold was the species that had most tickled her fancy. Not only did it have an attractive little golden yellow head— like a chrysanthemum with restraint—but apparently when planted near things like lettuce or tomatoes or cabbages, it kept the latter free from pests (*see* Garden/Summary/Contents: Chrysanthemums and Garden/Inhabitants: Slugs).

Mint: Like bluebells, mint had just sort of been around in massive bushes in Garden No. 1. They'd used it very occasionally in their cooking, but personally, she'd always had a vague prejudice against the stuff because so many handfuls were necessary to even get a hint of its taste. In any case, when no mint was to be found in Garden No. 2, neither of them had thought it particularly important to remedy the situation (*see* Garden/Contents: Bluebells).

Potatoes: Not just a few rows as with other vegetables, but a whole section of his garden had been reserved for various kinds of potatoes when they were living in the country. By the time they'd moved into the city, however, the joint potato consumption of the couple had dropped to the point where it was far more sensible to buy the few they needed than go to the trouble of planting masses of them out back (*see* Diet/Healthful: Potatoes).

Pyracantha: *See* Garden/Contents: Hydrangeas, Virginia creeper.

Radishes: *See* Garden/Contents: Carrots, Lettuce, Spinach.

Rhubarb: Even in her handkerchief garden, there'd been a patch of what she took as naturally occurring rhubarb. The amount in his country garden—planted or not—had been massive, and it had therefore been something of a mystery (at least to her) why they seemed to be rhubarb-less in Garden No. 2. But not a concern. The quantity of sugar generally required to make rhubarb palatable made it close to a no-no for a health-conscious eater like himself, and *she'd* never been that much of a fan to begin with (*see* Diet/Summary/Compulsive/Harmful: Sugar and Garden/Contents: Bluebells, Mint).

Roses: His love of roses had been profound, if discriminating (scentless roses, for example, were beyond the pale). In Garden No. 1, roses of one kind or another had festooned two out of three of the bowers, climbed up the front door, and figured prominently in many of the flower beds. For their second garden, the two had been modest and purchased only two small bushes. As the variety was chosen for the superb peach colour of the bloom, it was no small satisfaction to her that they'd actually flowered while he was still around (*see* Garden/Areas: Bowers).

Snowdrops: She'd always classified snowdrops with bluebells and crocuses—flora that was as natural a part of any garden as insects, though infinitely more pleasant. She (and possibly he—though she hadn't actually asked) had never had experience of a garden without them. Interestingly, in Garden No. 2, where she'd played a role in both planning and planting, she couldn't remember him actually planting snowdrops, nor was there a remaining packet of seeds or bulbs to tell her that he must have done. That notwithstanding, they'd duly appeared (*see* Garden/Contents: Bluebells, Crocuses and Garden/Inhabitants: Slugs).

Spinach: *See* Garden/Contents: Lettuce.

Thyme, creeping: As a variation in ground cover for the minipatio in their second garden, he'd obtained something called creeping thyme and planted it wherever the camomile didn't happen to be. Not wishing to hear the contrary, she'd privately decided that both the camomile and thyme were strictly ornamental and that there was absolutely no need for guilt over substituting their commercial equivalents in her cooking (*see* Garden/Areas: Herbs and Garden/Contents: Camomile).

Tomatoes: Strictly speaking, his numerous cherry tomato plants hadn't exactly been in their country garden, but rather in their own special gro-bags in the back porch area. Still, they'd (a) required just as much care as anything out-of-doors (and twenty times the watering) and (b) produced a crop that was light-years more delicious than any tomatoes on offer in supermarkets or farm shops. Indeed, *so* superior were the home-grown variety that in Garden No. 2 after his death, she had accepted a friend's offer of several small tomato plants and (when the time was right) had had her gardener plant them in a new set of gro-bags and ultimately bury bags and all in the vegetable patch.

Tulips: *See* Garden/Contents: Crocuses, Daffodils.

Virginia creeper: *See* Hydrangeas, Pyracantha).

Waterlilies: The waterlilies in his garden pond had intrigued her— not only for the perfection of their shapes and their beguiling colours, but for their cultivation. Assuming he would explain the latter when they got to that stage in Pond, Mark II, she'd never asked. When fate then decreed that such an explanation was not to be, she was left to concoct her own theory. The best she came up with was a process not dissimilar to planting rice shoots, though how one got waterlily shoots through the lining of the pond she could never figure out (*see* Garden/Areas: Ponds).

Weeping willow: In Garden No. 2, he had decided that a miniature weeping willow would look smashing next to the little pond. So it was that they had purchased one from the garden centre—a specimen so young that its little branches had stuck straight out instead of bending over to give one less an impression of weeping than of morning exercises. Indeed, once the tree was planted, she had been unable to hide her disappointment over the calisthenic branches and he had had to tell her not to worry—in time it *would* take on the characteristics of the species (*see* Garden/Areas: Pond).

INHABITANTS

Birds: Her knowledge of birds was, if anything, even more woeful than her knowledge of plants and flowers. Of the little group that either called at or resided in Garden No. 1, he'd pointed out crows, blue tits, blackbirds, sparrows, thrushes, and robins. Whether or not this constituted a complete list, the birdsong was very constant—especially in the milder months. An example that had particularly delighted them was a song that sounded uncannily like a ringing phone. He'd at least known it *was* a bird, though the first time they heard it he didn't tell her until she'd twice gone to pick up the receiver. In their city garden, the bird population seemed to have shrunk drastically to a pair of blackbirds, or else she was no longer paying attention (*see* Garden/Areas/Inhabitants: Wildlife).

Butterflies: *See* Garden/Areas/Inhabitants: Wildlife and Garden/Contents: Buddleia).

Frogs: Their genesis only slightly less fun than that of the waterlilies, a frog or two lived in or on the edges of the pond in Garden No. 1. They were small enough to hold in one's hand and, along with the goldfish, were in the enviable position of inhabiting the single element that his cat wasn't too keen to explore. She imagined he must have purchased the frogs when he got the goldfish, unless they'd sort of sensed on their own that a new body of water was in the neighbourhood and hopped over—admittedly, a less likely hypothesis (*see* Garden/Areas: Pond; Garden/Inhabitants: Goldfish; and Pets/Summary: Cats).

Goldfish: *See* Garden/Areas: Pond and Garden/Inhabitants: Frogs.

Moles: During their time in the country, moles were definitively classed as unwanted inhabitants. How to get rid of them, however, was less straightforward. He wasn't the type to seek a "final solution" like gas or shot—indeed, save the one time his cat Fluffy half-killed a small bunny and out of pure mercy he'd had to finish the job, she did not see him kill anything more complicated than an insect the whole time she knew him. No, he generally preferred to make things unpleasant. As soon as he saw a mound, he'd take an enormous shovel and bang away, invariably commenting (if she was watching) that in fact he wasn't doing anything worse to the little sods than giving them a headache (*see* Garden/Areas: Lawn; Garden/Inhabitants: Rabbits; and Pets: Cats).

Rabbits: Lacking all other proof, she would have known there were rabbits in their country garden solely by the half-dead creatures deposited at their feet by his cat. He'd offhandedly mentioned that the former (and their parents) hung out in the orchard, though he'd never bother to prove it. Come to that, he hadn't spoken of them as pests or in any way classed them with moles—that is, to be stunned into leaving the area. In fact, it was *they* who'd left first by moving to the city (*see* Garden/Areas: Fruit trees, Wildlife; Garden/ Inhabitants: Moles; and Pets: Cats).

Slugs: In her eyes, slugs represented at one and the same time all the obnoxious insects that nullified one's labour in the garden *and* the ultimate in nastiness. Had it been left to her, she would have resorted to the most deadly chemical to clear them out. But it wasn't, and his philosophy of organic gardening had favoured natural methods. As for the hapless slug that happened to slither into the back of their house (a fairly common occurrence when they were living in the country), such was the effect it and its slime exercised upon her that she would neither kill it nor help it on its way. Instead, she'd jump up and down shouting for him to do something—which he generally did (*see* Garden/Contents: Marigolds and Pets: Cats).

$\mathcal{H}$

$\mathcal{H}$ouse

Summary

During their time together, the couple occupied two residences. The first was a country house he'd purchased after his divorce and lived in for almost ten years. For her, living in the country was a new experience, involving (among other things) pigs—as opposed to people one *called* pigs for their revolting habits or cruel behaviour—as neighbours, and physically buying and handling one's own fuel. Not even the gas cooker had been attached to the mains, something she hadn't known until the night their dinner had stopped cooking. She'd reached for the phone. He'd taken the phone from her hand and gently explained that they used propane, actually; it came in cylinders; their current cylinder was empty and he'd get a new one in the morning. He'd then procured a little gas burner from somewhere, which didn't work too well either; they'd eaten their dinner half-cooked, and she had reflected on how precarious life in the country could be. She'd kept the reflection to herself, however. In both appearance and ambience, their country house was one of the most unusual dwellings she'd ever come across, and (with the proviso that she tended to view him as the only thing standing between her and likely death) a bona fide adventure to live in. That said, over the years *he* had come to resent both the effort and time the house and grounds required, and ultimately it was agreed that sooner rather than later they would move. The house they subsequently bought came (a) attached to every fuel source it could be attached to, (b) stuffed to the rafters with mod cons, and (c) a stone's throw from innumerable shops and bus routes. In fact, it even possessed something they *hadn't* looked for: the potential to be managed by her alone. If she could be thankful for nothing else after his death, it was that once again she was living somewhere she could comprehend, and that he'd remained fit until they'd completed the lion's share of the decoration and he'd been able to demonstrate how most things worked (*see* Biography/Joint: New York City; Garden: various; House/Challenges: Decor; House/Miscellaneous: Appliances, Chores; Illness/Summary/Last [His]/Experiences: Hospital, Nursing home; Love/General: Openness; and Transport/Summary).

ADVENTURES

Floor covering: Like so much else, the couple's philosophies of floors were in no wise similar. To her, you took floors as you found them: If they were awful, you covered them with a carpet, and if they weren't, you put a rug in their middle. To him, floors could be improved or even replaced. In the country, for example, he'd contemplated laying a wooden floor over the cement one in the kitchen and didn't in the end only because they'd left. When, however, their *second* kitchen floor turned out to be a patchwork of utility squares and uninspiring tiles, not to mention the only surface in the whole house not amenable to carpeting, the wooden floor that never was suddenly loomed again. Her heart sank at the thought of what faced them, but what the hell. They bought the necessary planks, stained and laid them, only to discover that the wood should have first been exposed to the central heating so it could shrink. As it was, it shrank *after* it was down—giving them less a floor than the pedals of an organ. Somewhat chastened (being a carpenter, he should have remembered about the shrinkage), he told her not to worry. They had plenty of other prepared planks, and these they would make certain *to* expose before using them as replacements. Which they did, though his illness had prevented them from actual re-laying (*see* Abilities/Summary/Do-It-Yourself and Work/His: Carpentry).

Purchase: Prior to meeting him, she'd had no desire to own property. The rules governing the buying and selling of houses in England appeared to her as only slightly less esoteric than those attached to membership in a religious cult, and anyway, she'd never had the money. During their time together, however, both of these circumstances changed. For one thing, he had been through purchases several times, and the prospect of undertaking one with a veteran seemed to render it less forbidding. For another, her mother had died unexpectedly and she'd come into a generous inheritance. Once in their new home and happily decorating, he'd declared that as house purchases went, theirs had been a snap. They'd had no need of a mortgage; they hadn't had to sell before they could buy; they'd got the place they'd set their hearts on; and they'd even had a few thousand knocked off the asking price because they'd paid in cash. To her, though, it had been everything she'd feared. The sheer labour involved in choosing a place, dealing with the mob that live off such occasions, finalising the deal, and then moving made her ask herself how the rest of humanity (who had to worry about financing as well) ever came through it sane. After his death, even more bizarre thoughts took hold, and she actually wondered if her whole relationship simply hadn't been a very circuitous means of getting her out of the unappetizing accommodations she'd rented into the smashing house she now owned (*see* Biography/Joint: New York City; House/Summary/Adventures: Sale; Money/Summary; and Wills/Summary).

Sale: The sale of House No. 1 had not been an easy business. Though they'd put it on the market before even starting to look for its successor, there'd been so many difficulties that they had already moved before it was ultimately sold. The principle difficulty seemed to be that it was timber and a bungalow—in her opinion, the very two features that gave the house its charm. Her opinion, however, counted little, since building societies in their neck of the wood weren't too keen on the combination and refused mortgages to one prospect after another. In fact, it was only after (a) a change of estate agents (with all that involved), (b) the discovery by the new agent of a surveyor with a bit of imagination and a heart, and (c) several months of worrying themselves sick about not selling the house before winter that the magic people with magic finances had appeared. To say the pair had been relieved would be an understatement. The unforgettable day the future owners had arrived to measure for furniture, and the wind was in the wrong direction and the pigs were stinking and one of them had looked at the other, smiled and exclaimed about the wonderful country smell, she—for one—could have kissed them and the pigs in that order. Stupidly, she'd relaxed after that, thinking everything was settled. It was thus her own fault entirely that she was unprepared when a sudden weak link in the buyer's chain looked like it might queer the whole deal just hours before they were due to take possession. It hadn't ultimately, though her heart had stopped along with everyone else's (*see* House/Summary/Adventures: Purchase).

Shed: On the third of the acre in the back of his country house, there had been several sheds of varying size. The largest of these he'd made into a workshop, while in smaller ones he'd kept considerable stores of wood, paintings and sculptures, and other miscellaneous items. Once in the city with nowhere near the same space available, the couple decided on a single shed large enough to provide both workshop and storage areas. This was completed before they'd actually moved, which was probably just as well considering that when the floor was being laid, the hose attached to the cement-mixer had burst and spewed cement on everything within a three-house radius. A shed drama they personally experienced, by contrast, occurred when the structure was already finished. Seriously underestimating the number of man-hours needed, the removal company they'd engaged believed they could pack the couple's possessions on one day and move them the next. The single man sent to do the packing, however, managed no more than a third and as the days stretched on, the number of his co-workers and their desperation to get the job over began to climb in parallel upward curves. Too professional to take it out on house contents, the men instead directed it toward the shed, with the result that tools, wood, paintings, sculpture, and such were simply dumped, very quickly turning the interior into a Do-It-Yourself bomb site. The amount of toil *then* involved for the pair to put the mess right was monumental. For weeks on end, they hauled around objects many times their own weight and size and built shelves with tools that had to be dug out from the rubble. Never in her life had she participated in anything like this kind of manual labour, and any pride she felt at the felicities of their interior decoration was as nothing compared to friends marvelling at the workshop cum picture and sculpture storehouse they ultimately created. That said, all degrees of pride were swamped by rage when, after all the sweat and angst, he was allowed no more than a few months to enjoy the shed before becoming ill (*see* Abilities: Do-It-Yourself; Biography/ Hers: Job [Bible]; House/Challenges: Decor; and Illness/Last [His]/ Reactions: Grief).

CHALLENGES

Decor: In the years before they'd met, he had created a singularly original house in the country. The exterior was white with windows framed in red and blue—not unlike the principal sitting room, with white walls and each of its three doors in a primary colour. The smaller sitting room off to the right contained a wood fireplace and was painted in a warm shade of pink. The enormous kitchen next to it was as far from one of those planned jobs as it could be containing (a) not a cabinet to its name (he'd removed them), (b) every pot and pan hung on hooks, (c) a stone sink the size of a sitz-bath, and (d) the first honest-to-goodness larder she'd ever seen. The bedroom had been done in horizontal swathes of blue and various pinks and roses; in the firemen red bathroom, he'd painted words and arrows on the inside of the door to indicate the loo paper holder. A smaller room off to the left of the sitting room was used as his studio and thus "decorated" with whatever designs he happened to be working on. Only a small room (again to the left of the sitting room) seemed to lack any special touch, but it was the only one out of six that did and was more than compensated by the American Indian designs painted on the back exterior. The first time she ever saw the house, she'd absolutely loved it; the second time, she'd begun to love *him,* and once living there, she'd concluded that anywhere stuffed with expensive furnishings that all matched was boring by comparison. Surprisingly (given what he'd done before), decorating their house in the city was to prove very different. The two had purposely chosen a place where not only essential work (such as rewiring or double glazing) had recently been seen to, but where some of the rooms and all the halls and landings were in good enough shape to be left as they were. Realising that (a) unfettered originality wouldn't have matched what was already there, or (b) along with all the sweat, he now wished to leave his previous style behind, or (c) both—with the exception of their bedroom, where the rolling swathes of House No. 1 were repeated (though this time in earth colours)—the two seemed to opt for ordinary handsomeness wherever they painted, put up shelves, or replaced carpets and lighting fixtures. Though in principle a bit disappointed, she was ultimately as happy with the results as he when the month they'd dedicated to nonstop decoration was over and most of the initial work completed. As to the bits remaining after his death (not to mention all the plans they'd had for further down the line), she often wondered when, if ever, they'd be finished. Indeed, just the sight of preshrunk floorboards waiting to be laid or kitchen cabinets still in place or the front door and back conservatory only half-painted or the empty space he'd left for the drawers in her wonderful mahogany desk was sufficient to reduce her to tears (*see* Abilities: Do-It-Yourself; Art/Concepts: Imagination;

Biography/Hers: Job [Bible]; House/Summary/Adventures: Floor
covering, Shed; House/Miscellaneous: Desk; and Illness/Last [His]/
Reactions: Grief).

Heating: During their first winter together, she'd found that instead
of a central heating system, which—with the merest thermostat
adjustment and service check—did its thing efficiently and
unaided, they had to rely on an antiquated monster that gulped
down unending supplies of something called Furnacite and then
required electric fires for a top up because it couldn't keep them
warm. Still, at least the two had been in agreement about using the
fires. The same could *not* be said, though, about the advantages of
an electric underblanket. The latter had been a signal blessing all
the years she'd been single, and, under the circumstances, she was
loathe to abandon it. For him, however, getting into an ice-cold bed
was a combination of some test of endurance and his very own
Madeleine, and he'd refused to discuss its reinstatement. Even
before the new owners rung late one night to say that the boiler
had blown up entirely (very embarrassing), she'd been patently
relieved when they'd moved into House No. 2, where central
heating—as the world understood it—existed. Less fortuitous was
the pretend coal fire (in reality, a gas contraption one ignited like
a cooker), which had had pride of place in their new sitting room. No
doubt recalling the lovely wood-burning fireplace they'd left
behind, he'd initially informed her that pretend coal was beyond
the pale and would have to go. Within a month of moving in,
however, he'd changed his tune and could only marvel at how
natural the flames looked. Both before and after his death, they'd
had the boiler serviced and declared in perfect working order. What
hadn't been looked at, though, were the timer and the two pipes
leading *to* the boiler, which—the very cold winter after he was
gone—conked out pretty much at the same time so that the
heating went on and off when it liked while the timer displayed
unearthly hours like 1:70 A.M. Happily, the gas people had been

very good and fixed it almost immediately (*see* House/Summary/
Miscellaneous: Chores).

Miscellaneous

Appliances: Every inch the technophobe classique, pre-him she'd
sought to own as few appliances as possible. Lifestyle-wise, this
had rooted her somewhere in the poor end of 1950, but she hadn't
minded. There was something perversely satisfying in being the only
one she knew without a video camera, VCR, answerphone, car,
computer, fax, washing machine, dryer, compact disc player,
dishwasher, or microwave oven. Once they'd met, however, with
the exceptions of the computer, which she'd subsequently bought,
and the fax, dishwasher, and microwave (which the pair had
considered de trop), she'd suddenly found herself appliance rich.
His attempts to teach her how to work everything had been slow and
uneven in result. She'd more or less caught on to the VCR (though
only to play videos, not record them), the answerphone, the washing
machine and dryer, and the compact disc player. Her mastery of
the video camera never seemed to last longer than the thing was in
her hands, and a car was irrelevant as a medical condition made it
sufficiently difficult for her to obtain a licence to put her off driving.
That said, they'd not worried too much, since ninety-nine percent
of the appliances had belonged to him, and he'd been around to
operate them. After his death, however, not only was she suddenly
faced with mastering the lot or being in *shtook,* but as most of the
items were quite old, she'd also had to cope with one thing after
the other starting to fall apart (*see* Abilities/Summary: Computer,
Photography; Garden/Summary; Illness/Chronic: Epilepsy; and
Transport/Summary: Car).

Chores: Right from the start, the couple had been scrupulous about
sharing the preparation of meals, washing up, and general
housework. Even gardening, in which she was little more than dumb

labour, extracted her equivalent of the hours he tried to put in. Certain chores, however, such as watering indoor plants or doing the wash, were somehow his exclusive province. Not that she wouldn't have watered everything in sight if only he'd told her how much and how often or that she didn't make a point of helping him hang the wash on the line whenever possible. In fact, without a single discussion it was accepted that *she* alone was to put away clean apparel as well as change the bedclothes. Perhaps the single task in their first house she couldn't or wouldn't do—aside from looking after his cat—was tend the solid fuel boiler. It was bad enough having to watch *him* continuously shovel Furnacite from the Black Hole of Calcutta where it lived, pour it inside a little compartment, poke at it, and later clean away the ashes before starting all over again. And this didn't even include the time he'd declared he was going to sweep the chimney. She'd fretted over how he was supposed to fit inside the flue right up to the moment he'd unearthed and joined together two halves of an extremely long "chimney" brush, stuck it up the fireplace, and begun to poke around. Indeed, such was her relief that she hadn't minded (much) as he and the entire sitting room turned increasingly black. Ultimately, his illness put an end to task sharing of any kind, though by then they were in House No. 2, which (because a professional cleaner was now doing the heavy stuff) was chore-heaven compared to where they had been (*see* Abilities: various; Biography/Joint: Rituals; Character: Laziness; Cookery/Summary; Garden/Summary/ Areas: Shrubs; House/Summary/Challenges: Heating; Illness/Last [His]/Experiences: Hospital, Nursing home; and Pets/Summary: Cats).

Desk: Prior to meeting him, she'd never had a study of her own—let alone a desk to go in it—but instead had made do with kitchen tables and miscellaneous shelves or drawers. This situation continued after they'd begun living together, as there had been no study as such in the country house for her to appropriate, and their desire to move had rendered impractical any notion of creating one. In House No. 2, by contrast, fitting up her study was given equal priority with getting his studio and the shed in order. A room was chosen and rapidly painted, festooned with shelves, and carpeted— all of which, while gratifying, were still but a prelude to the last, more eagerly sought decoration. Even before they'd moved, she'd known that he intended to *make* a desk for her and that he had just the wood for the job—a magnificent piece of mahogany some 10′ 6″ long, 20″ wide, and more than 1″ thick that he'd purchased thirty years earlier. Never in that time had the piece been touched, and (aside from size) she hadn't been too impressed with it on first viewing—an opinion she was to blush over once they'd actually cleaned and oiled it. In fact, the wood came up so beautifully that she'd been thrilled when he'd announced he could use the whole piece by cutting it into two unequal lengths in an "L" shape to go along the whole length of one wall and about three-fourths of a smaller one at right angles to it. Less thrilling was his insistence that helping clean the mahogany was to be her one contribution to the desk-making process, but no amount of protest could change his mind. Thus it was that on his own he'd hauled each length up a flight of stairs (a weight-lifting feat she'd thought was going to kill him), attached each length to its appropriate wall rather like a ledge, and finally positioned an electrical outlet above rather than below the desk so she could plug things in without difficulty. Even minus the two sets of drawers he never got to, it still had to be *the* most handsome desk in the Western world, though what ultimately touched her most was its sheer length—as if every inch represented his way of making up to her for every year she'd had no desk at all (*see* Abilities: Computer, Do-It-Yourself; Biography/Hers: Job [Bible]; House/Summary/Adventures: Shed; House/Challenges: Decor; House/Miscellaneous: Work area, His; and Work/His: Carpentry).

Settle: She'd be reminded of his profound admiration for medieval furniture each time they wandered through a church or stately home old enough to have some on view, and he'd stand rooted and speechless in front of every single example. When he'd first told her that he could reproduce it without much effort, she'd taken it as uncharacteristic braggadocio, but when he subsequently suggested constructing a variation of a settle for their new sitting room, she'd thought again. What he'd had in mind was a unit to replace a three-tiered table he'd specifically made to hold the gramophone, CD player, radio, and cassette player. While ingenious in its way, this table was constructed from ordinary pine and wholly utilitarian. He had, therefore, proposed a sort of shelf-cum-settle combination made from either mahogany, iroko, or whatever other hard wood might be lurking in quantity in their shed. From what she gathered of the concept, which—given that he hadn't the chance even to commit it to paper before becoming ill—was pitiably little, part of the audio equipment would have rested inside a compartment under the seat while the rest was to be on shelves at the same height as the back. Perhaps of all the furniture he was prevented from making, the would-be settle unit topped the list of those she most regretted (*see* House/Challenges: Decor; House/Miscellaneous/Work areas, His; and Work/His: Joinery).

Stained glass: To her surprise—since she'd traditionally thought of stained glass as a church feature—two stained-glass episodes were to figure in the decoration of their second home. The first involved a set of eight windowpanes (four 10″ × 16″ rectangles and four 17″ × 17″ squares) he somehow had in his possession. The rectangles were made up of twelve mini-squares of alternating rose, blue, and yellow; the squares of thirty-one mini-diamonds of the same alternating colours, with both shapes framed in a thin band of bright turquoise. Because he'd never before found a use for the panes and the glass was poor quality, the pair had initially left them behind. Once in their new home, however, he'd soon decided they'd be a very good means of keeping the sun out of his eyes when he was working in the conservatory. Thus had he retrieved the lot and varying the squares and triangles, fixed the panes over the tops of some of the conservatory windows to make a rather striking trim-cum-sunshade. The second episode had involved no windows and ordinary glass. While still in residence, the prior owners of House No. 2 had accidentally smashed the back door and offered to replace it with an exact duplicate. Not much enamoured of the original, the pair rejected the offer, began looking for a door of their own, and soon discovered that the only one available in both their price and aesthetic ranges came with clear rather than cloudy glass. Never daunted, they had bought it anyway, and he'd covered the glass by painting a simple country scene, which was then divided into stained-glass-ish sections by applying a sort of lead or lead substitute that came from a tube. The finished product was as far from a church window as could be imagined but still gratify-ing whenever the sun shone and its extremely vivid colours were projected onto the garden (*see* House/Challenges: Decor and House/Miscellaneous: Work areas).

Work area, His: In the country house, he had turned one of the bedrooms into his studio. Bar a few modest shelves, a tiny table, and a sort of easel that fitted to the wall, the room was absolutely bare—though the light coming in from the single window wasn't bad on sunny days. In the second house, he'd first considered the former-loft-turned-master-bedroom as a replacement because of its sets of dormer and ordinary windows, but then rejected it because of the two extremely narrow flights of stairs that constituted the only means of access. Instead, his new studio was waiting for him on the ground floor in what had probably been the dining room. Considerably larger than what he'd had before, the room also opened onto the longer side of an L-shaped conservatory, which meant he not only had the luxury of two separate areas for painting and sculpting but also perfect daylight and the ability to step back and look at his paintings from a distance. In such a wonderful space, decoration was supremely easy. The missing carpet and light fixture—elsewhere a disadvantage—were here a boon, as he would have had to remove them himself if they'd been left. Indeed, all that *was* required were several four-foot shelves attached to one of the recessed walls to hold his art materials; the fitted easel, which was placed on the wall opposite the conservatory doors; and a long shelf underneath it for paints and an impressive row of lights just above. The conservatory already had a shelf and sufficient space for his clay, plaster of Paris, modelling table, and sculpture tools and was considered "complete" with no more than the panes discussed above and a plastic ground sheet (*see* Art: various; Biography/Hers: Job [Bible]; House/Challenges: Decor; and House/Miscellaneous: Desk, Stained glass).

I

*I*llness

Summary
Not surprisingly (given that she'd lost Love No. 1 through illness), good health had ranked high among desired attributes in a partner. In this regard, his youthful appearance, strength, athleticism, and octogenarian parents had all augured well. Indeed, even after he'd admitted to being a possible coeliac, her surround of security bubble hadn't cracked. She'd simply assured herself that colitis wasn't necessarily life threatening and God wasn't about to zap her *twice*. All the same, after learning of his condition, the bubble did take on a different *character*, that is, instead of a single globe, it reshaped itself like an old-fashioned coffee percolator with the bottom, larger portion corresponding to her panic at each minor ailment he happened to mention and the top, smaller one to their joint indifference to the genuinely serious condition—at least until he grew so ill as to render indifference impossible. As to *her* state of health, whether it ever featured as significantly for him is more difficult to assess. As he hadn't experienced her many bereavements, she'd tended to doubt it. If anything, his greatest worries about her had had more to do with the threat of unforeseen accident than debilitating or fatal disease (*see* Attitudes: Hiking; Biography/Hers: Epilogue; Biography/His: Walk; Biography/Joint: Walks; Character: Youthfulness; House/Miscellaneous: Desk; Illness/Chronic: various; Love/Summary/General: Need; Self-image/Contributing to: Exercise; and Transport: Bicycle).

CHRONIC

Allergy: Allergies had always been a fact of her life. Her maternal grandmother had suffered from a veritable cocktail of them; they'd then skipped a generation only to reappear in herself and a number of her cousins. Looking back, she could not point to (a) a time during childhood when she *wasn't* going to an allergist (it was coming home from such an appointment that Mother had launched into her menstruation soliloquy); (b) ever testing negative to an allergen; or (c) the resultant injections bringing relief. The occasions when she'd been pronounced "cured" particularly stood out in memory—above all the time she'd started puberty and the change in her body chemistry had rendered the old allergens harmless but immediately replaced them with a brand-new set. Once an adult in the pre-him years, she'd pursued alternative remedies with as much conviction as her mother had invested in injections—and with as little effect. She had actually begun to wonder if what she really wasn't allergic to was the twentieth century when they'd met, after which she'd (eventually) gone to a Tibetan doctor and *presto!* Via a combination of herbal pills and special diet, *midseason* her itchy eyes, serial sneezing, and general wheeziness had all completely ceased (*see* Biography/Hers: Menstruation; Diet/Regimens: Tibetan; and Sex/Considerations: Odour, Taste).

Back pain: Considerable physical strength hadn't prevented him from damaging his back during the years he'd worked as a carpenter. By the time they'd begun living together, the problem had become so acute that he'd told her that he couldn't see himself continuing with carpentry much longer, and the pair had been grateful that as it happened, circumstances had allowed him to quit. Of course, even once he was no longer professionally hauling massive chunks of wood about, he was still the principal carrier for themselves—particularly during the decorating phase in House No. 2 (though he always wore his weight-lifting belt for support, and she insisted on carrying her share). Perhaps had lifting heavy objects been the only activity to avoid, he might have been all right. But, sadly, the demons of the back-disadvantaged could lurk anywhere—from installing a set of backseats in a mini-van to painting the ceiling in a bedroom. All and all, during their time together his back had hovered between an inconvenience and a misery—the solitary bright spot being his repeated avowals that making love relieved every bit of pain in the area and his undeniable friskiness afterward (*see* Art/Form: Sculpture; House/Adventures: Floor covering, Shed; House/Challenges: Decor; House/Miscellaneous: Desk; Money/Summary; Sex: various; Transport: Car; and Work/His: Carpentry, Joinery).

Colitis, ulcerative: During their time together, his pronouncements concerning his colitis were sparse, offhand, and inconsistent. In her eyes, they'd demonstrated a mind-set that ranged from putting the best light on things to virtual denial. As a rule, the pronouncements had two themes—either he'd admit to the condition but then declare that he had cured himself through a self-help diet, or he *wouldn't* admit to it because he claimed the doctors had said his symptoms were sufficiently atypical to rule out a definitive diagnosis. Whichever tack he chose, though, the same points always emerged: (a) colitis was present in his mother's family, (b) the one time he'd attempted to deal with the colitis conventionally, there wasn't the slightest doubt in his mind that the treatment would have done him in faster than the disease, and (c) eating certain things could and usually did have unpleasant consequences. After his death, she couldn't help wondering if he *had* persisted with conventional treatment from the beginning whether it might have prevented the disease from metamorphosing into colon cancer, which then spread to his liver and killed him. But this was the sort of gratuitous speculation often indulged in after a death and about as useful as observing: "If the grandmother had testicles, she'd be the grandfather" (*see* Biography/Hers: Epilogue; Biography/His: Leanness; Biography/Joint: Restaurants; Diet: various; Illness/Summary/Chronic: various; and Passions/Holidays: Christmas).

Epilepsy: Much as she employed the term *reincarnation* as a sort of shorthand for the simultaneous incarnation notion she *actually* subscribed to, "epilepsy" had become shorthand for a condition that—if unmedicated—produced symptoms very close to petit mal. The reasons behind the peculiar nomenclature reached back to the battery of tests she'd undergone both when the condition first appeared and then again in England. Exhaustive as these had been, they had only been able to reveal what the problem wasn't—such as a tumour or epilepsy. Even mumbling (the second time round) about likely brain damage during her birth had proved beyond confirmation, thus prompting her doctors to stop worrying about causes and deal exclusively with her symptoms, which they had done. She'd been impressed by such pragmatism and had decided to follow suit by thereafter calling the condition what it wasn't rather than launching into tortuous and unsatisfactory explanations (*see* Beliefs: Reincarnation; House/Miscellaneous: Appliances; and Transport/Summary).

Thrush: One evening—though she couldn't afterward remember how in the world the topic had arisen—a mutual friend had observed how cunnilingus could keep one and one's partner in a perpetual state of aural and vaginal thrush. Immediately upon this being uttered, the pair had exchanged a long, meaningful look. Once back home where they could talk, the two very soon agreed the following: (a) the friend was merely fishing—she didn't know, (b) whether she did or didn't, *they* knew and they'd have to abstain for a bit, which was unfortunate since neither could say for *how* long, though, and (c) maybe that wasn't necessary *after all* because they'd both already spent good money on remedies from the chemist (*see* Sex/Considerations: Taste; Sex/Involving: Mouth; and Sex/Realities: Kissing).

Experiences

Anesthesia: He was twice put under anesthesia during his last illness. The first time was when they removed his colon and the second when they tried to correct the problem causing his jaundice. His reactions to the anesthesia very closely reflected the progress of the cancer at the time of each operation. With the first, he was sufficiently awake on being brought back from the recovery room to make funny faces when she first saw him, whereas the second time he didn't come round for several days. Indeed, after his death, she learned that he'd almost died while they'd been performing the second procedure (*see* Illness/Last [His]/Experiences: Blood transfusion, Operations, Stoma).

Blood transfusion: One way or the other, the number of blood transfusions he was given in hospital quickly went into double figures. They were (a) first started as an antidote for the anemia, (b) then required during each operation and immediately thereafter, and (c) finally—when it was acknowledged that he was beyond any further form of treatment—given as a sort of top-up before he was sent home (*see* Illness/Last [His]/Experience: Operations and Illness/Symptoms: Anemia, Jaundice).

Cancer, liver: While the first discovery concerning his liver (that a shadow was present) had engendered unusual tranquillity between the two, confirmation of inoperable cancer in the organ prompted a fantasy comfort scenario. The scenario had its origin in his statements about how the removal of his gut had given him a new lease on life (since all his grief and angst had always been stored there and now he was a happy man) and ran as follows: (a) their love had removed the reasons for his unhappiness and by extension, his cancer, (b) the ileostomy had deprived it of its locus, (c) even allowing they were in a vital organ, not simply did the tiny scattered nodules described to them sound more like acne than cancer, but as they now lacked their former raison d'être (*see* [a]), they were more amenable to treatment than the cognoscenti credited. Combining as it did total holistic plausibility with a happy ending, the scenario probably kept the two going until the onset of his jaundice and second admission to hospital (*see* Illness/Chronic: Colitis, ulcerative; Illness/Experiences: various; Illness/Symptoms: Jaundice; and Love/Summary/General: Tranquillity).

Diagnoses: Looking back, there seemed to have existed an uncanny connection between the growth of all the diagnoses offered about his worsening health and the growth of the cancer. In fact, after his death, she'd occasionally wondered if physical cancer didn't have a mental counterpart in the proliferation of notions regarding its recognition and/or treatment. Whatever, the multiplication of *their* diagnoses had started at home. With increasing frequency as he grew more tired and ill: (a) one of them would come up with the reason why, (b) the reason would be eagerly taken up by the other, (c) a remedy from the health shop or chemist would be sought, (d) the latter would either have no effect or else help only briefly—and the process would begin again. Later, when all diagnoses were in the hands of professionals, there was none of the initial certainty that had accompanied the earlier inspired guesses of the pair. Instead, diagnoses were (a) offered tentatively, (b) generally corroborated, (c) eliminated prior to the remedy stage until, ultimately, (d) one unquestionable cause *was* established—whereupon the resemblance to his cancer ended (*see* Diet: various and Illness/Experiences: various).

Doctors: The sheer diversity of doctors at every stage of his illness had, for the pair, brought back memories of buying her computer or investing his money—except that this time, choice wasn't involved, but simply keeping up. Whatever the number of doctors, though, there wasn't one who didn't soon grow fond of him as a patient.

However he'd claimed to have acted in the past, his natural amen-ability (in *her* presence, anyway) seemed to preclude complaining and bolshy behaviour and ensure he went out of his way for others—from cheering a succession of fellow patients to helping students by allowing them to take his medical history, to even—when finally, he was past all treatment—acting somewhat abashed, as if he'd let the side down. After his death, out of all the doctors who'd been involved, she'd been unable to forget a particular female consultant who, as chance would have it, somehow became the invariable bearer of disastrous tidings. So completely did visits from the lady and then the lady herself come to represent the next nail in her darling's coffin that eventually she began to shun her and, when that wasn't possible, to openly show her dislike (*see* Attitudes/Summary; Abilities: Computer; Character: various; Money: Invest-ment; Illness/Chronic: Colitis, ulcerative; and Illness/Experiences: various).

Drugs, conventional: His compliant attitude toward conventional drugs during his final illness represented, in her opinion, a surprising reversal of attitude. Previously, he had condemned conventional colitis medication—calling it more damaging than the illness—and more than once told her how, when his condition was first diagnosed, he had unilaterally withdrawn from the course of treatment prescribed for him. Now, it seemed, presented with what were probably quite similar—if not the same—drugs, he behaved like a total pussycat and took everything without so much as a murmur. Though she would have never dreamed of calling the *volte face* to his attention, privately she *had* wondered about it and after his death decided the following: (a) by the time he was admitted to hospital, the colitis had progressed to a point where he could no longer pretend that the self-help diet had cured it, (b) overall, he was too ill to be either independent or skeptical, or—taking a different tack—(c) discontinuing the medication the first time round had been an aberration (*see* Illness/Chronic: Colitis, ulcerative and Illness/Experiences: various).

Hospital: The pair were extremely fortunate vis-à-vis his two stays in hospital in that a first-rate teaching hospital happened to exist in their city, and it was within walking distance of House No. 2. Proximity was to prove a particular blessing, since hardly a day went by when he wasn't asking her to bring or remove art materials, magazines, items of clothing, or the like. These daily treks, plus the nine or ten hours she would try to spend with him once there, had the effect of turning the hospital into as much of a home for the pair as the place they'd moved into some six months earlier, and each soon became as familiar with its various wards and units as the rooms in their newish house. Overall, his comments about (and her memories of) the hospital were uniformly positive. Both the treatment he'd received and the kindness at every level of staff had been outstanding—particularly when she thought of the small fortune either of these would have cost in her own country. In light of this appreciation it was, therefore, a signal of disappointment that after his death she could not bring herself to go near the place—not even to thank the score of people who'd looked after him (*see* Art/Concepts: Imagination; House: various; Illness/Experiences: various; and Love/General: Tranquillity).

Nurses: Whereas the degree of good feeling he was able to cultivate with his doctors was limited by the brevity of their visits, nurses were around for all the hours of their shifts and (in theory, anyway) under no such restrictions. This gain in time, however, was offset by number: three or four nurses per shift; two or three shifts; Nurse X going off, on, or returning from holiday, never mind that he was to occupy at least three different floors of the hospital during his illness. With all that, it did appear that he could keep them all straight in his mind. For her, though, individual personalities began to blur after the number had topped eight, and a composite nurse emerged in their stead: (a) eminently efficient, (b) not just friendly, but quite happy to have long talks with him about his art, (c) willing to go out of his or her way when he didn't ask, and (irrelevant to the above but interesting nonetheless) (d) usually good-looking (*see* Illness/Last [His]/Experiences: Doctors, Hospital, Nursing home).

Nursing home: After his second discharge from hospital, she had tried to look after him at home. While being a caregiver had been a challenge from the start—particularly as his final illness had been her caring *debut*—yet it was as nothing compared to this final phase. Not simply was the mental anguish unrelenting and more acute than any physical pain she could imagine, and the exhaustion overwhelming, but (to her horror) as the days went by, she actually began to *want* him dead—though in the Newspeak she used with herself it came out as wanting to end the ordeal for them both. That said, she still might have seen it through to the end had the physical situation not also got beyond her. In short, though he could do little at this point bar lie in bed semi-conscious, every conscious moment he *did* have, he would want to get up to go downstairs and she had to restrain him. When, finally, this happened several times in the early hours of one morning, she gave up the struggle and asked for help. All nearby hostels being full up, a complicated rota of district nurses was proposed to cover the twenty-four hours of each day— the usual procedure in such cases. She'd taken one look at the list, however, and quickly realised that in the state she was in, there was no way she could interact with so many new people and decided to put him in a nursing home. Fortunately, a very agreeable one happened to be as close to their house as the hospital—*with* places available—and it was here, two days after his admission, that he'd passed away (*see* Illness/Last [His]/Experiences: Blood transfusion, Doctors, Hospital).

Operations: By successfully removing the diseased bowel with its payload of carcinomas, his first operation (the ileostomy) had equally removed the centre of his angst. This new sense of well-being was as obvious from his initial rapid recovery from the operation as from his comments to that effect. Indeed, had complete recovery depended merely on the ileostomy (and appropriate follow-up treatment), he might well have been spared for a few more years. As it was, he was already back home—taking daily walks up and down their road and doing small household tasks—when the liver cancer asserted itself and he became jaundiced. His second operation (to relieve the pressure on the liver that was causing the jaundice) was only partially successful and, anyway, academic with regard to the final outcome (*see* Illness/Last [His]/Symptoms: Jaundice and Illness/Last [His]/Experiences: Anesthesia, Blood transfusion, Cancer, liver).

Stoma: During his first stay in hospital, *stoma* ("an artificial opening made into a hollow organ, [referring] especially [to an opening] on the surface of the body leading to the gut") was to become far more than an exotic addition to the pair's vocabulary. Granted, prior to his final illness both had heard of individuals who'd had their bowel removed and were, for the rest of their days, dependent on pouches rather than on the normal means of evacuation. Perhaps the actual topic had even been discussed during their time together—she couldn't later be certain. There was, however, little question that discussion did not begin to approach the experience of having it happen to *you* or your partner. Their own experience had begun the night before his operation with a cheery booklet about what living with a stoma meant and his being asked to dress so that the best location for the stoma in relation to his everyday clothing could be determined (leading her to muse, incidentally, if perhaps *now* he might be more inclined to wear the looser trousers she'd always advocated on fashion grounds). Then came the operation and a whole new world of (a) pouches, (b) *flanges* (the adhesives that held the pouch to the body), (c) diet, (d) rules for travelling—particularly abroad, (e) sustained marketing assaults from every pouch manufacturer in Britain, and (f) an entire hospital department dedicated solely to helping people like himself. The new world had even treated them to an amusing experience before his ultimate relapse. He was already home from hospital and still (surgically) recovering in leaps and bounds. One day he'd actually felt well enough for the two to go for a coffee at a nearby café. Everything was fine until he'd put his hand in his pocket, turned white, and whispered that he thought the catch (by which the pouch was emptied) had opened. Without another word, he'd rushed off to the toilet and she'd sat there trying to think what the booklet had said about possible accidents in the beginning and if the worst *had* happened, how to get home as unobtrusively as the situation allowed. A few minutes went by when, smiling, he'd sauntered out of the toilet, sat down, and informed her that what he'd felt hadn't been the catch but merely his set of housekeys. Then there had been her own feelings about it all. She could remember as a small girl being taken for some reason—perhaps because her mother was already a widow and had had no one else to go with—by the latter to the home of a family friend whose husband was dying of cancer. The man had had half his face cut away; it had been absolutely awful and she hadn't been able to wait to leave. Happily, *he* hadn't been mutilated in any obvious way, and she'd felt confident that pouches were something she could as well get used to as he. In any event, such speculation was to prove superfluous (*see* Biography/Joint: Travel: Illness/Last [His]/Experiences: Operations and Self-image/Contributing to: Dress).

X ray: Even by the time of his first admission to hospital, he'd become so thin that at times she would wonder why they even bothered with X rays—surely a penetrating look would have done as well. That said, of all the tests and nonsurgical procedures he went through, being X-rayed was probably the one the pair least minded, as it was neither intrusive nor gruelling. It was also something *she* didn't have to flee from—as flee she invariably did when they were taking his blood. On the contrary—if she happened to be present when he was scheduled to go for an X ray, she'd happily volunteer to take him to the department, wait, and then take him back again.

Symptoms

Anemia: About three or so months before he died, he had become so anemic as to be unable to move about without considerable difficulty. At first, it wasn't understood what was causing the anemia, and he was given an initial course of iron tablets, which simply passed through his body and gave him terrible cramps. After a fortnight, his blood count was again tested; it was seen that the anemia was worse, and concern about the condition as well as other symptoms led to his first admission to hospital (*see* Illness/Last [His]/Symptoms: various).

Breathlessness: One of the first signs of his anemia was difficulty in mounting the two flights to their bedroom in House No. 2. He'd just about make it up the stairs and then have to sit down for a minute or two to catch his breath. After a while, a brief pit stop on the first-floor landing was also required. That such breathlessness might be a cause for worry was not, at the time, a tenable hypothesis for either. At first, he'd asked her over and over whether she also didn't become breathless, and when finally they'd established beyond question that she didn't, both of them had then moved on to flip observations, such as (a) he must be getting old, after all or (b) he'd obviously become spoiled by living too long in a bungalow. Even when the flippancy had grown as worn as himself, still neither was prepared to believe that one day he wouldn't be bounding up the stairs like a gazelle (*see* Illness/Last [His]/Symptoms: Anemia).

Jaundice: After his first operation, he would generally spend most of the day resting in the garden. As it was spring and the weather quite pleasant, she was only too happy for him to be outside. Indeed, on going out to check on him one afternoon, she was delighted to see what looked like a bit of colour from the sun on his face and body. As the days passed, however, the "suntan" began to go distinctly yellow, and it wasn't long before the pair realised that in fact it was jaundice, most likely caused by the cancer in his liver. While a second operation and several blood transfusions managed to partially correct the problem, his normal complexion never returned (*see* Biography/His: Fair colouring, Leanness and Illness/Last [His]/ Symptoms: Weight loss, various).

Weight loss: At least six months before his final illness, they'd been walking down the road when she turned to face him and was struck by how thin he'd become. She'd said nothing at the time, preferring to believe that he'd *always* been like that, more or less. He, likewise, hadn't referred to what was happening—at least until he began to look like a skeleton and one morning getting out of bed, he couldn't resist a brief, deprecating remark. Otherwise, only his reluctance to have her touch him provided any clue to his feelings about his deterioration. As for herself: could she somehow have cut off strips of her own flesh and given them to him, she wouldn't have hesitated (*see* Attitudes: Health maintenance; Biography/His: Leanness; Love/General: Monogamy; Love/Specific: Caressing; Self-image/Contributing to: Exercise, Muscle; Sex/Considerations: Dependence, physical; and Illness/Last [His]/Experiences: various).

REACTIONS

Acquiescence: When she could no longer pretend otherwise, to herself or him, and accepted not only that he wasn't going to recover but that he hadn't much time left, she'd naturally assumed that they would talk about it. Indeed, up to this point there had been absolute solidarity between the two. Together they'd (a) faced every iota of bad news, (b) passed through initial tranquillity, (c) woven comfort fantasies, and (d) when they were told that conventional medicine could do no more, relied on alternative medicine to save him. Yet now—when it was most vital—a stage was reached whereby neither could bear to speak directly to the other about what was happening. Granted, one morning he did tell her of a dream he'd had the night before in which he was saying good-bye to everyone, and—perhaps more naturally for him—undertook a series of the most harrowing death drawings, though she'd only discovered these afterward. None of that, however, *nor* her own weeping on absolutely everyone else's shoulder, was a proper substitute for final, loving conversations (*see* Art/Styles: Experimental; Attitudes: Ecology; Love/General: Tranquillity; Illness/Last [His]/Experiences: Cancer, liver; and Illness/Last [His]/Reactions: Strategies, alternative).

Grief: *See* Art/Concepts: Imagination; Biography/Hers: Epilogue; Garden/Inhabitants: Birds; House/Adventures: Shed; House/Challenges: Decor; Illness/Last (His)/Reactions: various; Love/Summary/General: Need; Music/Types: Opera; Passions/Art: Redon, O.; Time: Past; Transport: Public; and Work/Hers: Writing.

Strategies, alternative: On the one hand, the various green beliefs of the couple (particularly his ability to heal and his faith in self-help diets) and on the other, the all-too-natural reaction of *any* individual in similar circumstances, made alternative strategies an inevitable last resort. Such strategies were the last topic in regard to his illness the two were to discuss, though interestingly, the former had probably been in the minds of both even prior to hearing that he was too far gone for either chemo- or radiotherapy. Indeed, during his first hospital stay and at his request, she had purchased several books dealing with nonconventional attitudes toward cancer. The logic in these books had sounded absolutely *right,* and the life extensions and/or outright cures referred to—if one was to believe them—undeniably impressive. So it was that when the final prognosis had been pronounced, they had decided to enroll in the one and only centre in Britain practising a philosophy and treatment along the lines of those advocated in their books. Indeed, she'd actually sent along a deposit and was looking into how best to get there when the centre (having reviewed their application form) informed her that, unfortunately, their treatment was not intended for anyone as sick as himself—and that had closed the final door (*see* Abilities: Healing; Attitudes: various; Diet/Summary/Regimens: various; and Illness/Last [His]/Reactions: various).

Love

Summary

As she'd understood it, successful love went thusly: (a) you met and were strongly attracted; (b) at some point, you fell in love with the object of your attraction—which, while very nice, was not the mortar with which one built a life together so that (c) you then began *to* love instead of *be* in love. After that she was on shakier ground as neither of the two important men in her life had survived past *c*. In the latter relationship and for as long as he was alive, neither had ever doubted that their feelings would (or could) diminish. Contrary testimony from long-termers about a make-or-break crisis after ten to twenty years, and one's initial love mutating into a passive if still important sentiment—when not drying up altogether—was always listened to politely by the pair, then countered with the observation that if after twenty years *they'd* grown tired of each other, they'd both be too decrepit to do much about it. Privately, the two believed that meeting in middle age had probably made them immune to the usual run of love dissolvents. And then he'd died and all speculation concerning their future became irrelevant. Instead, she dwelled on memories: his daily warnings that she should watch out for cars when crossing the road (or anything else that might harm her); his declarations that living with her was a perpetual holiday and his patience with her stubbornness and overbearance; her conviction that somehow she could ultimately wipe away his feelings of inferiority and her inability to walk by wherever he was without touching him. Above all, she remembered the real joy that had accompanied every activity they'd jointly undertaken, and how, for a time, they'd been convinced that the power of their feeling for each other might actually defeat his cancer. Even allowing for the softening effect of memory, their two years together seemed very close to an idyll, and the observation of others that one day she would be *grateful* to have had them perhaps more than just the lame consolation she now took it for (*see* Abilities: various; Attitudes/Summary; Beliefs: Miracles; Biography/Summary/His: School; Biography/Hers: Job [Bible]; Biography/Joint: various; Character/Summary: Humourousness; Cookery/Summary; Garden/Summary; House/Summary; Love/General: various; and Illness/Last [His]: various).

GENERAL

Anniversaries: Having decided not to marry, the pair dated their anniversaries from their first meeting. For him, this had occurred on the day they'd been introduced, whereas for her (since they'd exchanged no more than a few words at the time) it was their first lunch together. In the end, the couple compromised on a date somewhere in between, and when the time came, duly celebrated with a long weekend in Swanage. Aside from the gambol on the cliffs, her most vivid memory of the occasion had to do with an exquisite bouquet of flowers waiting in their room when they'd checked in. Each time she'd looked at it, she'd wondered what it was doing there, as it was patently out of place in their modest little B&B. Close to an hour must have gone by before she'd at last noticed a card and realised that the bouquet had come from *him*. Typically, he'd said nothing the whole time and the overwhelming surge of love behind the hugs and kisses she then showered on him had been mixed with a real pang at her own obtuseness (*see* Attitudes: Marriage; Biography: various; and Love/General: Sentimentality).

Boundaries: Having repeatedly heard in the pre-him years how important it was for a couple to allow each other space, once they'd begun living together she couldn't help noticing that the couple unit *she* belonged to did a great deal *à deux:* baking, cooking, days out, evenings out, gardening, holidays, house decorating, household chores, sewing, shopping—be it for clothes, food, or materials connected with their home or work—and walks. Even more ominous was the ability (even without a shared activity) to spend any amount of time in each other's company without becoming bored or irritable. That in fact they appeared to be the *least* spaceless couple in England was a proposition she'd anxiously lived with until a bit of time had passed and she'd at last recognised (a) the amount of solo time each sought with long-standing friends (and he with his daughter); (b) the graceful retreat of one or the other to a different part of the house when the occasional difference of opinion over television programmes required it; and (c) how much both of them relied on her daily sojourns to the library for a guarantee of mutual noninterference during working hours and *his* liberty to wander through the entire house if he wanted to listening to Radio 4 (*see* Abilities: various; Art: various; Biography/Summary; Cookery/ Summary; Garden: various; House: various; Love/Specific: Arguing; Music/Types: various; Passions/Miscellaneous: Jazz; and Work/ Summary).

Decision-making: The genesis of decision-making for the pair provides an interesting example of theory versus practice. Togetherness notwithstanding, her love for him had had an irrational, maternal streak about it and had initially inclined her either to take all decisions upon herself (thereby sparing him the worry) or else leave them to him entirely (thereby boosting his self-esteem). Once they'd begun living together, however, neither inclination was to prove especially realistic. Not only had his temperament and philosophy de facto precluded cutting her out of the decision-making process, but her own common sense had (once she'd actually paid it a bit of attention) soon indicated that excluding *him* would probably achieve more in the way of gross insult than mental relief. That joint decision-making had thus been the only viable option in the circumstances (*and* a damned good idea) is indicated by the couple's agreement level, which had generally averaged in the ninetieth percentile (*see* Abilities: Finances; Attitudes: Women; Character: Organisation; Cookery/Summary; and Love/Summary).

Discovery: Certainly from the first or second meeting, not only could she say that she loved him but why. So blatant had been every one of his love-inducing qualities that her subsequent discovery of the *whole* man, not to mention herself as his partner and both of them as a couple had come as a surprise. Early on, she'd decided that probably the best way of coping with this avalanche of new information was via simple categories (i.e., Concrete or General as to its nature and *Hers, His,* or *Joint* as to whose it was. A sample list might thus read: CONCRETE: *Hers:* Discovering he was a healer and his various methods as an artist; *His:* Discovering her organizational abilities and her staying power at New Year's Eve parties; *Joint:* Experiencing the holiday in Greece and putting their shed to rights. GENERAL: *Hers:* Exploring how far his love of the earth extended and the roots of his inferiority complex; *His:* Understanding the connection between her background and social skills and how she came to accept or avoid physical challenges; *Joint:* Assessing outside opinions of themselves as a couple and the mechanism behind their similarity of taste both in modern and traditional art. That said, the biggest discovery of all—at least for her—was to what extent raw love turned another human being into one's curriculum (*see* Abilities/Summary: various; Art/Summary: various; Attitudes: Ecology, Hiking; Biography/Hers: America, New York City; Biography/His: School; Biography/Joint: various; Character: various; and House/Adventures: Shed).

Emergence: During their time together, the affection between the pair was of a quality to prompt—to varying extent—the emergence of each from his or her psychic "shell." In her case, the latter had been the subject of a poem written just before the death of her first love. It began: "Do you know/how much you love me/is how much I love me/or how much joy derives/from reinstatement/to the ranks of One Desired?" The poem went on to speak of her intense envy of individuals whose self-worth was buttressed by the feelings of a beloved and how he had enabled her to leave behind her former roles of outsider and have-not. The exact poem could have been written ten years later during her second relationship—the single addenda being that this time, the self-worth created by the new attachment was strong enough to survive the passing of its source. In both instances, the experience had not touched upon her public behaviour. *His* emergence, by contrast, had been obvious enough to provoke comments from some long-standing friends about his increased confidence and volubility. Even meeting new people—a dread activity for him if ever there was one—increasingly seemed to involve less angst beforehand and a semblance of enjoyment when it happened (*see* Biography/His: School; Character: various; and Self-image/Summary: various).

Happiness: *See* Beliefs: Miracles; Biography/Summary/Hers: Job (Bible); Biography/Joint: New York City; House/Summary/Challenges: Decor; and Sex: various.

Monogamy: Before he became ill, she would occasionally compare his still-muscular buttocks and thighs to her own. Though she'd been quite slim as a young woman and was still in fairly reasonable shape, there could be no doubt that those two areas showed her age. Once, on an evening when there'd been a particularly generous helping of perfect female bodies on the telly, she'd had to say it. He'd replied that bodies like that bored him (they showed nothing of life) and, putting his cheek against the curve of her belly, added that every time he saw an attractive woman, it only made him desire her the more. Though there was nothing wrong with *his* body, she would have said as much of him (*see* Attitudes/Summary: Health maintenance; Biography/His: Leanness; Biography/Joint: Courtship; Character/Summary; Love/Summary; and Sex/Involving: Stomach).

Need: The needs of the pair changed considerably once they'd met—moving from the general to the specific. Very quickly, each one began to need the other not simply for what *any* "other" would have brought to the relationship, but for what only he and she could offer. Indeed, so dramatic became his proclamations that he wouldn't know what to do if anything ever happened to her, she'd almost been glad that if one of them had to die, it had been him. Not that she'd imagined herself as stronger, but the numbers were in her favour. As against his single experience of death (a grandmother some fifteen years earlier), she could weigh in with a dead father (in girlhood)—and then a lover, stepfather, and mother. In fact, when *his* death then brought the total to five (the final four in a scant ten years), she'd felt her status as a bereavement veteran began to approach those of unfortunates living in areas afflicted by war or natural disaster. Thus it was that for all he'd meant to her, she'd always stopped herself parroting the proclamation back to him and instead silently wished that for many years to come, the subject of *either* of their deaths might remain academic (*see* Biography/Summary/Hers: Epilogue; Biography/Joint: Grandmothers; and Work/Hers: Writing).

Openness: Though the pair generally sought to be as open as possible with each other (and the subject never arose) she'd always surmised that he probably had kept a few things from her simply on the basis that she'd kept a few from him. And why not? Indiscriminate honesty, in her opinion, carried a damage potential that far outweighed all the theoretical virtues of truth-telling. Anyway, if it was important for each one in a relationship to have his or her own physical space, surely it was hardly less important that they also have their own thoughts—either for self-reference or to spill to a friend. That, of course, was always allowing that the thought in question wasn't some earth-shattering biggy—like not informing your "other" you could no longer stand to look at his or her face (*see* Beliefs: Reincarnation; Character: Sensitivity; Illness/Last [His]/ Reactions: Acquiescence; and Love/General: Boundaries).

Pleasure: Pleasure had been an unequivocal core element in the couple's time together—and not just pleasure as sensuous enjoyment. He also lived by a philosophy that put into practice pleasure's other definition: delight. His notion of lovemaking, for example, was extremely broad, including almost every activity they jointly undertook. This had seemed odd to her until she'd recalled two friends—a couple who were both keyboard musicians. The first time she'd watched them give a joint concert, the affinity of their playing had struck her as much the most intimate thing she'd ever seen. Pleasure for the pair hadn't necessarily required shared activity, however. Until he became ill, just seeing him or hearing his voice after even the briefest separation was enough to excite active pleasure in her. His subsequent death, however—particularly as he wasn't the first lover death had taken—left her wondering if it wasn't foolhardy to make *any* individual the nucleus of one's pleasure. When they died, not only did delight and sexual pleasure disappear entirely, but even the small pleasures left the survivor—such as those involving hearing, sight, or taste—were invariably diminished (*see* Abilities: various; Biography/Summary/Hers: America, Jew; Biography/His: various; Cookery: various; Garden: various; House: various; Love/Summary; and Sex/Considerations: Pleasure).

Proximity: When they'd first arrived at her mother's flat in New York on that fateful visit, she'd viewed the sleeping arrangements with misgiving. The imposing double bed she had known from all the years of her mother's second marriage had, after her stepfather's death, been replaced with something vaguely resembling a Napoleonic chaise longue. Though barely wide enough for *one,* aside from the floor or a sofa divided into too many sections to be comfortable, it was the only sleeping area available. Even her dying mother had been sufficiently concerned to ask how they were managing on such a narrow bed. But managed they had. For two solid months, they shared no more than thirty-nine inches between them. Granted, the chaise longue had had to be repositioned so that neither side of it was touching a wall, and once or twice there'd been accusations of space hogging, but overall (and to her profound relief) it had been rather cozy and proved the two could weather the closest proximity without ill effect (*see* Biography/Summary/Joint: New York City and Love/General: Boundaries).

Rescue: *See* Biography/Summary/His: School; Character: Diffidence, Self-effacement; Love/Summary/General: Emergence.

Sentimentality: The pair had been pretty sentimental. Even before the flowers at Swanage—indeed, even before they'd got together—he had sent her one of the largest bouquets of red roses and baby's breath she'd ever seen. Such was its mass that a neighbour had had to give her several vases, as not only didn't she have one big enough to hold it all but even her supply of small vases was insufficient. Another time, she'd noticed some sketches he'd done of them tucked up in bed together. These were lying neglected on his studio floor and she'd picked them up and said he should keep them. A few days later, he'd put a handsome frame around the sketches; written, "To my darling—, the love of my life" on the back; gift-wrapped it; and presented it to her. And then, of course, there had been her fabulous desk. As a rule, *her* displays of sentimentality were more predictable and heavy-handed. Christmas, Valentine, and birthday cards to him overflowed with long, overemphatic descriptions of what he meant to her as well as exclamation points strewn about like so many streptococci; and the only way she could restrain herself from buying him the entire world as a gift was by pressing him to tell her what specific thing he wanted. His reactions to such gush were generally (and characteristically) low-keyed (*see* House/Miscellaneous: Desk; Love: Anniversaries; and Sex/Summary).

Sympathy: *See* Abilities: Spelling; Attitudes: Marriage; Character: Sensitivity; Cookery/Summary; Diet/Summary/Healthful: Roe, Whitebait; Diet/Regimens: Tibetan; Garden/Summary; House/Miscellaneous: Chores; and Illness/Last (His)/Symptoms: Weight loss.

Tranquillity: The sense of tranquillity the couple had always taken for granted prior to his illness found actual expression during its course. He'd already gone to hospital and the two had just been informed that a scan of his liver had shown up a shadow, which might well indicate cancer. The consultants, junior doctors, and nurses had then moved on, and they'd looked at each other. He'd told her not to worry; she wasn't going to get rid of him that easily. He had everything to live for, and anyway what they felt for each other was strong enough for him to pull through. He'd even smiled and said he looked upon the whole thing as a challenge. The shared feeling of tranquillity at that particular instant had been overwhelming. Her dread had dissolved, and in spite of how sick he was, he'd appeared almost radiant. Though ultimately he'd been wrong, the intense power of that moment—of the peace they'd not only brought each other throughout the relationship, but could summon even at such a time—had remained a fact of her life (*see* Illness/Last [His]/Experiences: Cancer, liver and Love/Summary).

Trust: Little secrets notwithstanding, she'd trusted him absolutely—as she believed he'd trusted her. Vital areas of mutual trust, such as remaining faithful, never cheating or knowingly causing hurt had (during their time together) not merely been assumed but taken as a bedrock of the relationship. That said, she was well aware that affection on its own did not necessarily drag that sort of trust in its wake. There had to be other things present, like morality, kindness, and lack of chauvinism—all of which he'd possessed in abundance.

And though (like tranquillity) they'd never actually talked about it and so she couldn't be sure, she'd imagined him likewise building up his own trust equation with whatever parts of *her* character he'd held to be appropriate (*see* Attitudes: Marriage, Women; Biography/Joint: Meeting, first; Character: Kindness, Morality; and Love: Emergence, Monogamy, Openness).

Understanding: Understanding in relationships seemed to come in two varieties: (1) a sort of knowledge one possessed about the character of one's partner and (2) a nice thing one offered the latter out of love. While the force of the couple's feelings for each other had initially convinced each that there wasn't much he or she didn't know in *(1)*, it hadn't taken very long for experience to disabuse them. Chronic instances of him consuming a plate of roe or remaining absolutely mute at a social gathering; of her once *again* forgetting what he'd told her only thirty seconds previously about that little shoot not being a weed or being adamant about not camping—even in their back garden—had been more than sufficient to demonstrate to both that there were parts of the beloved's psychology eternally beyond comprehension. *(2)*, in comparison, had seemed resistent to inexplicable behaviour—indeed, more intertwined with affection overall—as to put far less strain on the givers (*see* Biography/Joint: Walks; Character: Kindness; Diet/Healthful: Roe; and Garden/Summary).

SPECIFIC

Arguing: She'd often heard it said that if a couple insisted they never argued, they were either indifferent to each other or lying. That notwithstanding, when *they'd* begun living together she'd vowed to herself that she would do everything in her power to avoid arguments. But her power hadn't been up to much or else it was something beyond anyone's power, like vowing never to breathe. Thus, argue they *had,* over a whole potpourri of topics such as (a) her sloppy work during the painting of Bedroom No. 2 (when she had thought she'd been doing rather well); (b) his nail biting; (c) her chronic attempts to include him in conversations with third parties; (d) whether or not to go to the top of the Empire State Building; and (e) the feasibility of pacifism. At the beginning, each time they'd had words she'd been ready to cut out her tongue until eventually she came to see that it was *all right:* They still loved each other, and the world wasn't going to end. Even so, the efforts of the pair to be as amenable as possible probably averaged higher than the norm (*see* Abilities: Communication, verbal; Beliefs: Pacifism; Biography/ Joint: Empire State Building; Character: Sensitivity; and House/ Challenges: Decor).

Caressing: Coming from a (reputedly) demonstrative race, she'd always taken for granted that one had physical contact with the people one cared for and that the amount of that contact was in rough proportion to the amount of affection one felt. Given that she had never before loved another human being to the degree she loved him, it was perhaps genetically inevitable that she'd seek to caress him whenever she could. Once she'd asked him if he minded, and he'd said no, it was wonderful—particularly as he'd never before been with women who were physically affectionate apart from bed. Indeed, he'd responded to her like a flower to sunlight so that soon he was caressing her as well until there was a period when they could hardly pass each other without some sort of embrace. While that calmed down after a bit, up until shame at what the cancer was doing to his body made him shun physical contact altogether, they'd found it hard not to be in each other's presence without a little hug or squeeze of the nearest available arm (*see* Biography/Summary/ Hers: Jew; Illness/Last [His]/Symptoms: Weight loss; Love/Summary; and Self-image/Contributing to: Muscle).

Laughter: During their time together, the couple had laughed a great deal. He, for example, could be extremely funny—something she'd first become aware of on their second date. They'd been walking down the street and for some reason (or perhaps none at all), he'd started talking in an uncanny Scots accent. She'd laughed and had assured him—when he'd then asked her—that she didn't mind such behaviour. On the contrary, it reminded her of her dead father, whose antics she had sorely missed while growing up. Instances of her inducing laughter in *him* were less successful (to wit, the disastrous introduction of her "funniest film in the world") or—like the giggles she'd invariably succumb to after one or two glasses of wine—unintentional. Perhaps the importance of humour for the pair is best illustrated by something that happened after he'd died. She'd been at home watching a video of a Chinese film and must have half dozed, though she continued to hear the accompanying music. Suddenly, he'd appeared and begun prancing around—as only he could—but in time to the music as if he heard it, too, and was attempting to cheer her up. While, not surprisingly, the attempt failed, yet she'd been struck that even death hadn't deprived him of his humour (*see* Beliefs: Afterlife; Character: Humourousness; and Passions/Cinema: Cinema).

Showers, joint: Though respective experiences of joint showers in the pre-her or -him years were not spoken of, the two had seen enough of them in films to make the procedure seem like a desirable way to get clean. As with so much else, however, disillusion was swift. After several attempts, the pair had had to conclude that either shower stalls in films were about six times the size of those allotted to ordinary human beings or else actors—because paid fabulous sums of money—didn't actually *mind* (a) bumping into each other, (b) freezing when not directly under the spray; (c) having lather dry all over them, or (d) running the risk of breaking their necks when trying to change places. Perhaps they even used a soap that never slid out of one's hands. As for adjourning to the shower for *sex* as well as washing—well, stand-up sex was tricky in the best of circumstances and ultimately demoralising when soap and water

turned one's single back support into a slithery mess (*see* Sex/
Realities: Intercourse, Positions).

Sleeping together: However broad one's definition of lovemaking,
the act of sleeping together was nothing to sneeze at. An actual
presence beside you; the warmth and comfort your other gave out
when you held each other acted like a magic bubble one could wear
through the day. At least, *she'd* worn it every day: She hadn't been
sure (since she hadn't been his first live-in bed partner
[as he'd been hers]) if his reactions were equally rapturous. Although she'd told herself they might well not be and she didn't mind,
in fact, she *had* minded sufficiently never to bring herself to ask
him (*see* Biography/Hers: America; Love/General: Openness; and
Love/Specific: Pleasure).

Talking: Very early on, the couple made it a rule to talk everything
over. Given that she had an infinitely bigger mouth than he, it might
be supposed that she'd talked and he'd listened, but that hadn't
been the case. During their time together, decisions on anything at
all were always jointly discussed; she listened to his opinions, life
story, fears, and ambitions and even reined in her chronic story-
telling, as it was pretty obvious she didn't need stories to impress
him and anyway, he soon knew most of them. Indeed, every time
he'd assure her that never before had he been able to tell anyone as
much as he told her, she'd believed him (*see* Abilities: Communication, verbal, Finances; Character: Charisma; Illness/Last
[His]/Reactions: Acquiescence; and Love/General: Tranquillity).

$\mathcal{M}$

$\mathcal{M}$oney

Summary

Via the unexpected death of her mother and the inheritance that followed, the two came into enough money to live comfortably. Via *his* unexpected death and yet another inheritance, she acquired the means to promote his work on the scale she felt it merited. The deal seemed to be (a) a loved one taken and (b) loot given in return, though *b* didn't *always* follow *a* and (c), namely, informing whatever was doing this to *stuff* the loot—she wanted the people, not actually entering the equation. During their time together, the pair had had occasion to recall the first-ever mention of money in their joint presence. Her mother had been visiting; they'd all gone out for a meal one evening when apropos of nothing, the former had suddenly turned to him and said: "My daughter is going to be a rich woman one day. What are your intentions toward her?" Having been forewarned that Mother was an aficionado of the "I'm-an-Octogenarian-Thereby-Entitled-Nay-*Expected*-to-Utter-Totally-Outrageous-Remarks" School, he'd chuckled softly and declared he was committed to her for life. From her position under the table, she'd shed a grateful tear—both at his composure and the response. Far sooner than any of the three would have imagined, the money had materialised. As it turned out, Mother had considerably overestimated how much she was worth, and even her overestimation was light-years short of what the world's genuine wealth holders would have termed *rich* (*see* Abilities: Finances; Biography/Joint: New York City; House/Adventures: Purchase; Illness/

Chronic: Backache; Love/General: Need; and Work/Hers: Writing, and Work/His: Carpentry).

Bills: Bills—of one sort or another—had tended to rain upon the couple far more than ever they had on her alone in the pre-him years. Mini the Moocher generated its own cloud; then there was the house insurance, taxes, utilities, and the usual variety of bills, which—even when paid in a single go—still required a modicum of their attention. One way or another, it had seemed to the pair as if payments were never done with, and she—for one—wouldn't have minded getting a psychological jump on them via a calendar that showed when annual, semi-annual, quarterly, or monthly ones came due. But he (no doubt imagining their daily expense list sufficient for the purpose) had never been keen on the idea, and it hadn't come to pass (*see* House/Miscellaneous: Appliances; Money: Budget, Credit, Taxes; and Transport/Summary: Car).

Budget: Looking back, she couldn't recall them ever sitting down and making up a budget per se. Once settled in their second home, however—and at his instigation—the two had begun keeping a daily expense list to show how much they were spending per quarter. Privately, she had doubted if in fact it had showed anything of the sort simply because assigning (and sometimes having to divide) amounts into columns marked Daily, Weekly, Quarterly, Household, Non-household, and Miscellaneous (read: It-doesn't-go-anywhere-else) was probably beyond the mathematical ability of the pair. That notwithstanding, she'd always enjoy the moment when they sat down to tote up the daily outlay. Not only was it a pleasant way to review the day's activities, but at the end of every quarter she'd love to hear how little they'd spent (though the latter was something she could have told him *without* lists, since early on she'd recognised that, like herself, he wasn't generally extravagant) (*see* Ability: Finances; Character: Morality, Practicality; and Money: Savings).

Credit: Having earned his living as a carpenter, he had inevitably relied on credit to keep both business and self going. She, by contrast, had had the advantage of a tiny but reliable sum her whole time in England and had always looked upon credit as something external to herself. Indeed, she was probably one of the few people she could think of who'd acquired credit cards as a means of identification rather than an aid to buying. When, eventually, she *did* begin to charge a few things, they were never so dear as to require serial payments. During their time together, the pair had been in the fortunate position of being able to continue paying bills in full. Indeed, the arrival of Visa or Access statements through the post invariably prompted the observation about both companies going bankrupt if they'd had to rely on customers like themselves (*see* Character: Morality, Practicality; Money: Bills, and Work/His: Carpentry).

Dollar: When she'd *first* arrived in England, the pound-to-dollar exchange rate had been around £1.00 to $2.33. Subsequently, not only had the pound never again approached even the $2.00 mark, but for a brief period the two currencies had actually hovered near par, thereby causing her to wonder if Britain wasn't turning into a new Weimar Republic and she oughtn't to go out and buy a small tower block or something. For his part, previous American associations had habituated him to the dollar both as concept and object, though (like most Europeans) he never *had* understood why all bills (regardless of worth) were uniformly green—thus maximising the possibility of mistaking a larger denomination for a smaller one. After a bit of reflection (not to mention sheepishness at ever having thought that all non-American currencies looked like play money), she couldn't think why, either (*see* Biography/Hers: America).

Inheritance: *See* Money/Summary and Wills: Estates.
Investment: In the pre-him years, she had become convinced that

ethical investment was obligatory for anyone with spare cash and a tender conscience. He had agreed—or rather she *believed* he had, since looking back, she couldn't actually recall him expressing an opinion one way or the other. The subject had first arisen after the sale of the country house. Given the aggravation the latter had entailed, the pair were not a little dismayed at what was now incumbent on them just to divest themselves of the proceeds. For sheer multiplicity of choice and assumed savvy, the whole business rivalled buying a computer and perhaps exceeded it for throwing in the unexpected. One bank officer, for example, had looked the two of them up and down, decided they couldn't possibly have more than a few thousand to invest, taken more than an hour of their time, finally asked them the amount and, on hearing that in fact they had considerably more, then informed them he wasn't their man, and that they'd have to begin all over again with someone else. Another had assured them that his institution's promise of ethics could conveniently evaporate if they *really* wanted to put their money into something nasty. Ultimately, they'd opted for a private individual who'd been knowledgeable enough to steer them to what they wanted, even if ruefully smiling all the while at their financial innocence. That said, in less than a year this very same man would himself be converted to ethical investment, though—admittedly— less for the goodness factor than his discovery about certain ethical funds being among the best performers in the industry (*see* Abilities: Computer; Attitudes/Summary; Character: Morality; and House/ Adventures: Sale).

Savings: About six or so months after the installation of the daily expense sheet, he'd announced the following: (a) they were generally spending less than their quarterly income; (b) the surplus was savings, wasn't it? and (c) perhaps instead of automatically applying it to the next quarter, it might be a good idea to deposit it in a separate account, which could be used for "holidays, etc." It had sounded like a great idea until she'd remembered that they already *had* an account ("Household") that covered "holidays, etc." In any case, the tortured calculations generally employed to arrive at expense-sheet totals probably made the latter's value as an indicator of anything (save the folly of *further* complicating a bookkeeping system already beyond them) dubious at best. Not wishing to get into a long discussion, however, she'd said nothing but instead smiled noncommittally and prayed he might forget the whole thing (*see* Abilities: Finances; Love/General: Openness; and Money: Budget, Credit).

Taxes: As a couple, both of them had paid taxes of one sort or another in Britain while she also paid taxes to the United States. In every case, calculating the amounts owed was left to professionals, since their own efforts—while no doubt rich in mirth potential for Inland and Internal Revenue Services alike—could never have guaranteed that ultimately they wouldn't have got stung for a lot more than they were expecting. The wisdom of such a policy was repeatedly borne out during their time together. Never were their taxes (a) too much higher than they'd vaguely reckoned, (b) burdensome, or (c) beyond their means (*see* Money: Bills, Budget, Credit, Savings).

*M*usic

Summary

Without question, music played a considerable role in the lives of the pair both before they met and after. Using the categories of Musicality, Instruments, Singing, Playing in Public, Exotic Tastes, Concert Attendance, and General Reliance On, a preliminary picture of these roles is possible to construct. 1. *Musicality:* She had actually taken composition lessons for some years, though more with the intention of sharpening her ear for language than making a career in music. Indeed, even had composing *been* her goal, she was too numerically illiterate to ever master the degree of musical notation the former would have required. As to improvising *at* the piano, she could produce simple arrangements of well-known tunes. He, by contrast, had been a natural musician—even on "her" instrument. That is, without ever having learned how to read music *or* play a piano of any description, he had repeatedly sat down at their digital keyboard and produced webs of sounds that were wholly original to himself and astoundingly rich in texture. 2. *Instruments:* As far as she knew, both his proficiency on the recorder and talent on a whole assortment of drums were self-taught. First and foremost, he'd been a jazz drummer and the impressive kit that had had pride of place in the sitting room in House No. 1 and the "music room" in House No. 2 had been in regular use right up to the time he became ill. She had had years of piano lessons in classical music, though the secondhand piano she'd acquired during the early part of her stay in England had been in too poor condition to take when she'd moved in with him in the country and was never properly replaced. Along with piano, she'd also spent several years studying the flute and a few months dabbling in a Chinese instrument called the *cheng*. 3. *Singing: See* reference for "Voice" in Biography/Joint: Voice. 4. *Playing in Public:* While he'd been a member of a jazz band during his teens, for reasons never revealed to her he had absolutely refused to play in public thereafter. She, too, had long ago forsworn any playing in public, though the reason for *her* reluctance was traceable to the stark terror she'd experienced (and the conclusion it wasn't worth it) preceding her one and only performance, namely, a piano competition during girlhood. 5. *Exotic Tastes:* Before the pair had met, he had visited Zimbabwe while she'd spent several months in Japan. Not surprisingly, the music of both those areas became their respective though not sole concerns (to wit, he likewise loved Indian music and she, Chinese). Sadly, the efforts of each to turn the other one into a musical convert of the parts of the world he or she favoured bore little fruit, perhaps because the time in which the conversions were attempted was so brief. 6. *Concert Attendance:* Concertgoing had not been a major social activity for the two. The few concerts they did attend were usually in classical music because she loved it dearly and such concerts were relatively plentiful compared to gigs offering the kind of modern jazz that were *his* baby. When, however, the opportunity to hear the latter *had* presented itself (as in New York when they'd gone to Carnegie Hall to hear Sonny Rollins), it was pounced on by both with equal enthusiasm. 7. *General Reliance On:* To her, music was like coffee or chocolate. In one form or another with the possible exception of songs in English, which could be distracting if she were writing, it had to be present whenever she was on her own. He, in comparison, while an avid radio listener by nature, would instinctively head for stations where talk was the staple and music the little morsels in between. Indeed, he'd probably been more interested in music as an event requiring all his attention than as background noise (*see* Art/Concepts: Incubation; Biography/Joint: New York City, Pianos; Diet/Compulsive/Harmful: Chocolate, Coffee; Love/General: Boundaries; Music/Instruments, various; Music/Miscellaneous: Music room, Types, various: and Work/Hers: Writing).

INSTRUMENTS

Bongos: He'd had two sets of these, one extra small (only four inches high) and the other more or less what she considered to be usual in size (closer to six inches). While she certainly could recall him having a (very impressive) go more than once on the bongos during their time together, it apparently must have been on the smaller set, since the skin on one half of its larger brother had been torn.

Cheng: The purchase of a *cheng* (an eighteen-string Chinese zither) dated from pre-him days—specifically, her intense Chinese music period. Despite a parallel purchase of a vast number of cheng tapes at the time so she could hear what it sounded like played correctly, the thing had remained beyond her. Reasons for this inability ranged from insufficient strength in her fingers to the fact that it hadn't come with a case (nor could she ever find one)—thus making it impossible to carry the cheng to the one man in London who might have taught her how to play it. Sadly, by the time she finally *could* have gone for instruction (because living with him had given her access to a car), the strings had gone, and she'd lost interest. Too impressive to get rid of, early on the cheng had entered a second incarnation as a display object—first in her own home, then in their bedroom, and finally in their music room (*see* Music/ Summary/Miscellaneous: Music room; Transport: Car).

Congas: Next to his beloved drum kit, he'd probably had the most recourse to the congas. In fact, early on she'd discovered the following: (a) he could continue a "spot" on them for what seemed like hours, (b) he used all parts of his palms and fingers, (c) he often did different things with each hand simultaneously, and (d) he was able to vary the rhythm at will. She had not appreciated the skill involved in all of this until he'd tried to teach her a few of the techniques involved. No matter how precise the instruction, how innumerable the examples or determined her effort, the most she could manage was a boring two-hand tap, which tended to last about eight seconds (*see* Music/Summary: Drum kits).

Cymbals, finger: He'd possessed *one* finger cymbal—thus leading her to speculate if (a) the one for the other hand had gone lost or (b) he possibly thought one was the correct number. On further consideration, she'd decided *b* was improbable as—with one or two exceptions—he'd seemed to know about and be able to play or convincingly improvise on every instrument in their house (*see* Music/Instruments: Rattle, Xylophone, hand).

Drum: Of all the drums he'd owned, this particular one was notable in that she could never recall him playing it, touching it, or even referring to it when showing off his collection to outsiders. Not that it hadn't asked for attention in its way being about twenty inches in diameter, antique looking, and (the once or twice she'd tapped it with her fingers) sounding like a bass snare drum. Its lack of use had reminded her of her cheng, though unlike the cheng, it had initially been kept out of sight until the move to House No. 2, when he'd fastened it to the wall just over the digital keyboard in the music room (*see* Music/Instruments: Cheng and Music/Miscellaneous: Music room).

Drum kits: Along with the drum kit referred to in the Summary, he'd kept an older one stored away in the attic of House No. 1. She hadn't even known of its existence until they'd been on the point of moving, and he'd decided it should be sold. Her single memory concerning that other kit was of the young boy who'd agreed over the phone to buy it and then brought his mother along for protection when it was time to hand over the money. The sight of them both had been only slightly less touching than the twenty minutes worth of playing hints thrown in by the vendor before mother and son had departed (*see* Character: Kindness and Music/Summary).

Drums, Zimbabwe: This was her own name for four drums ranging in size from eight and one half to twenty-two inches high, and covered with a variety of skin or membrane heads. Despite being made of wood or else an unidentifiable frame covered with skin, to her eyes they'd all looked sufficiently ethnic to assume they were African, which, of course, meant from Zimbabwe. That said, unlike the xylophones, he'd never actually *told* her they'd come from there—not even during the times she'd been treated to demonstrations of how they sounded (*see* Music/Instruments: Xylophone, hand and Music/Summary).

Flute: She had taken up the flute in pre-him days and during the first year had been unquestionably enthusiastic about the instrument and her progress. What a pleasure to be playing something one could actually carry from room to room (not to mention the really super pieces by Debussy, et al. awaiting her once she became good enough). By the year's end, however, she'd reached a sort of plateau beyond which she couldn't budge; Debussy disappeared forever from the horizon, and her lifelong preference for the piano began to reassert itself. After all, with a keyboard one (a) didn't have the keys so near to one's nose that one had trouble seeing which was which;

(b) wasn't required to indulge in the unhygienic practice of semi-spitting into an aperture to produce a sound, *or* (c) called upon to struggle setting up a music stand every single time one wanted to play because there was no place to leave the damned thing assembled (*see* Music/Summary/Instruments: Recorder).

Maracas: While the small brown-beige gourd with seeds or whatever inside it could technically be called a maraca, it was more like a rattle than any Latin American maracas she'd ever seen. Not merely was there only one of it, but that one had a group of holes (on one side of the bell) that had been partially covered with a piece of white tape. Whether (a) these holes were where the filling had been inserted, (b) leaving the holes uncovered meant the filling was at risk, thus necessitating the tape, and (c)—unlike the finger cymbals—it *came* singly were things she wouldn't have minded knowing, though not enough to bother finding out about after his death. The one thing she would risk saying was that, as with so many of his instruments, he'd likely got it from Zimbabwe (*see* Music/Summary/Instruments: Cymbals, finger).

Piano, digital: *See* Biography/Joint: Pianos; Music/Summary/Miscellaneous: Duets, Sound production.

Rattle: This consisted of twelve balls arranged in rows of three, with rope edging on top and bottom, which one shook. Beyond that, however, she could say little else about it. He'd never used or even referred to the rattle during their time together, and whatever information he'd had about the thing had died with him (*see* Music/Instruments: Cymbals, finger).

Recorder: More than once she had seen him pick up the recorder and play it with the greatest of ease. While she could never remember what the tune had happened to be, she *was* fairly certain that it was never the same one each time and that he was surprisingly adept at flourishes. While always enjoying his performances, she'd also resented them a bit because of her tribulations with the flute. Interestingly, she'd never asked him to have a go on the flute and he'd never volunteered (*see* Music/Instruments: Flute).

Xylophone, hand: He'd had three of these, all fairly small and of different designs. They appeared to consist of metal tongues; a wooden soundboard; a bridge; a metal bar for restraining the tongues, and rattle or buzzing attachments. She presumed they were played by depressing the tongues with the fingers of both hands, though she'd never seen him actually do it. She did know, however, that all three came from Zimbabwe because she'd overheard him say as much to several interested guests at one of their Christmas parties (*see* Music/Summary/Instruments: Cymbals, finger and Passions: Holidays: Christmas).

MISCELLANEOUS

Contemporary music: If his affection for *The Firebird* had been something of a surprise, his attitude to the shards of contemporary music that occasionally surfaced on the radio had knocked her sideways. On her own (and she considered herself a sophisticated listener), she'd generally tune out after a few seconds, only vaguely guilty about not giving whatever it was much of a chance. If they were both there, however, the music was listened to. Indeed, not only had he always given it his full attention—no nodding off or doing something else at the same time—but once it had finished, he'd then tell her how much he'd enjoyed it or (most remarkably) lapse into the particular silence that indicated he was too affected to immediately put his reaction into words (*see* Music/Miscellaneous: *The Firebird* and Music/Types: Classical).

Duets: More than once during their time together, he had suggested a duet with him on drums and her at the digital keyboard. While she would have liked nothing better, generally she couldn't bring herself even to try, or (on those rare occasions when she'd force herself into an attempt) she'd invariably give up after a few moments—thereby prompting sighs on his part and (as he'd launch into a solo) a slinking exit from the music room on hers. Such uninspiring behaviour had its roots in her musical history. Never having played with another musician in the pre-him years, she equated group playing with performing (i.e., a major taboo). Added to that, their digital keyboard possessed considerably fewer octaves than the piano she'd grown up with, so that every time the music indicated notes that weren't there, she couldn't think what to do other than stop. She would have gladly confessed all of this to him had he ever been churlish enough to demand an explanation, but of course he hadn't been—which had only made her feel even more wretched. Ultimately, the word *duet* had passed out of his vocabulary (*see* Biography/Joint: Pianos; Character: various; Love/General: Pleasure, Openness; Music/Summary/Instruments: Piano, digital; and Music/ Miscellaneous: Music room, Sound production).

Firebird, The: One day, apropos of a topic she couldn't later recall, he had declared Stravinsky's *Firebird* to be one of his favourite pieces. Though not the bombshell of his reaction to contemporary music—after all, *The Firebird* was accessible and exciting—still she hadn't been expecting it from a combination jazz buff–classical music avoider like himself. Indeed, in her mind the announcement had had the effect of lifting *The Firebird* from its purely musical perch into a quasi-mystical example of the affinity underlying their love. So it was that the mystical and musical were to merge (at least for her) when several weeks later he purchased the work on CD, and they sat down for the first time to listen to it together (*see* Love/Summary/General: Discovery, Pleasure; Music/Summary: Contemporary Music; Music/Types: Classical; and Passions/Miscellaneous: Jazz).

Music room: Unlike House No. 1, where instruments had been parked here and there, House No. 2 was sufficiently roomy to dedicate one room to nothing save the pair's music-making. At least, that had been the intention prior to moving. After the move (and for reasons stated above), the room witnessed little music beyond his drum solos, and even these were far less frequent and prolonged than they'd been in the country house, where he'd been absolutely certain that no one could hear him. Still, once the two sets of shelves had gone up, and all the musical instruments owned by the pair artistically arranged on them and on the walls and carpet, it had become impressive enough to evoke little cries of admiration from however many visitors happened to see it (*see* House/Summary; Music/Instruments; Cheng, Drum; Music/ Miscellaneous: Duets, Sound production).

Rhythm: *See* Music/Summary/Instruments: Bongos, Congas.

Sound production: Sound production fell into two categories: (1) creating it oneself through playing an instrument and (2) listening to the sound others recorded or performed. In category (1) would have come their principal instruments, his drum kit and her digital piano. The kit was a Ludwig—a real honey that required no more than a talented drummer like himself to bring it to life. On the other end of the scale was her digital "piano"—less an instrument than an electronic abortion in that no matter which of the buttons marked "Piano," "E. Piano," "Vibraphone," "Organ," or "Strings" one pushed, one invariably got the aural equivalent of straight vermouth passing for a martini. Regarding (2), together the pair probably possessed the full range of gadgets from radios to gramophones to tape decks to reel-to-reel jobs to a fascinating little CD player (no bigger than the CDs themselves), all of which came with amplifiers and speakers that were interchangeable as long as one knew about the little holes in the back of everything, which—praise God—he had done. Perhaps the single other aspect of sound production that stuck in her memory had to do with what he'd taught her about making a tape of every non-CD one loved enough to play ad nauseam (*see* Biography/Joint: Pianos; Music/Summary/Instruments: Piano digital; Music/Miscellaneous: Duets, Holliday, B.).

M USICIANS

Baker, C.: *See* Passions/Miscellaneous: Jazz.

Beiderbecke, B.: Among his impressive collection of jazz and blues tapes, she'd come across one or two of Bix Beiderbecke, though as he was generally anti very early jazz and during their time together never played or spoke of them, she'd assumed the tapes were primarily there for purposes of completeness. Personally, she harboured a soft spot for Bix. She got a kick out of the sound he and his band had produced—so ancient one almost had an impression of what jazz might have sounded like in the pre-record era. But even more fascinating were the Beiderbecke lyrics, which were anti-lyrics—about absolutely nothing. In fact, given the hard-boiled and even obscene songs that would begin to be heard not too many years later, one was left wondering if Beiderbecke had lived on the same planet let alone in the same country as the greats who would follow him (*see* Music/Summary/Musicians: Smith, B.).

Collins, A.: Whatever his overall affection for Albert Collins, during their time together that affection had focussed on a single number only. In it, Collins is heard in a heavy guitar solo whilst a female chorus protest, though always in time to the music. The women begin softly, trying to get Collins's attention by calling "Mr. Collins, Mr. Collins" immediately adding "Please, Mr. Collins. Don't play that *loud,* Mr. Collins!" As the solo continues, they get increasingly agitated and are soon shouting the lines as a refrain. It's all to no avail, however—bar the last few chords, Collins gets to the end at exactly the same volume if not louder than he began. Each time he heard the number (and he'd listen to it often), he'd chuckle—and so did she. As the ultimate putdown to every complaint ever made about loud music, it had to be unique.

Ellington, D.: Duke Ellington had been a favourite with the pair. Not merely had both of them actively listened to cassettes, CDs, and records of his music, but he was the one composer who at times could inspire more than simple listening or accompaniment. These times had had to do with when the couple gave a party. Before anyone arrived, he'd put on the score to the film *The Cotton Club* and invariably launch into a solo dance routine—either grooving slowly to "Creole Love Call" and "Mood Indigo" or energetically bopping to "Drop Me Off in Harlem" and one or both of the "Cotton Club Stomps." As early on she'd decided that (a) his style of dancing was every bit as individual and endearing as the way he walked and (b) the natural high spirits behind it were a good indication of his contentment, never had she found the routines either repetitive or boring (*see* Biography/His: Walk; Character: Humourousness, Youthfulness; Love/Specific: Laughter; and Pets: Cats).

Hampton, L.: One day in their country house, she'd been in the kitchen busy writing when suddenly a fabulous drum solo began to emanate from the sitting room. She'd stopped what she'd been doing and had just sat and listened, thinking (a) he was playing, (b) while she'd known he was good, she hadn't realised he was *that* good, and (c) it was criminal that anyone who could produce such sounds should absolutely refuse to play in public. When the solo finally ended, she'd walked into the sitting room saying "Boy, that was really impressive!" only to discover that though he was sitting at his drums, the drummer had been Lionel Hampton (who she'd always imagined had played nothing save vibes) and the source of the music, an extremely superior disc. It had been an awkward moment for them both (*see* Music/Summary/Musicians: Morello, J.).

Holliday, B.: Like Ellington, not only did the couple both have Billie Holliday on cassette, but a few of the cassettes happened to be identical. This proved to be fortunate, since even when they first got together, as she had played her supply to the point where Lady Day was beginning to sound distinctly loopy. Not worrying about it, she'd simply reached for his—whereupon she had had her first demonstration in preserving one's favourite tracks—he made two copies of every one of *his* Holiday cassettes, and in no uncertain terms ordered her to stick to the copies (*see* Music/Miscellaneous: Sound production and Music/Musicians: Ellington, D.).

Morello, J.: When one day she'd asked who, in his opinion, was the greatest drummer of all time, the answer he gave was Joe Morello. She'd never before heard the name, but beyond Ringo Starr and Gene Krupa she didn't know too many drummers any-way and was willing to be instructed. Sadly, it never happened. She couldn't remember him playing anything of Morello's during their time together—or perhaps he had done so and she hadn't known. Either way, after his death she'd made a point of listening to the one cassette of the drummer she could find. There was no denying it was impressive, but nothing on it (in her opinion) came near to the startling Hampton solo she'd heard a year or so earlier (*see* Music/Musicians: Hampton, L.).

Smith, B.: So taken had she always been with Bessie Smith that years before they'd got together, she'd actually composed a song about her called "The Empress of Blues Blues" and given it to a semi-professional jazz band she knew. That none of the band members (bar one) could read music had not, to her mind, detracted from the song's value as a badge of commitment. He, by contrast, had not been much of a fan. She couldn't remember him playing his few cassettes of Smith's music, even though there's little doubt they wouldn't have had a good laugh if he had done so, as the lyrics to many of the songs were so obscene. Certainly, the one or two *discussions* the pair had about Bessie repulsing a Klu Klux Klan attack by shrieking curses at the attackers and not being treated by a white hospital after an accident and thus bleeding to death before she got to a coloured one had been pretty engrossing (*see* Music/ Summary/Musicians: Beiderbecke, B. and Work/Hers: Writing).

TYPES

Classical: Family legend had it that she was introduced to classical music at the age of three days, when her bassinet was wheeled in front of the radio in time for a performance of Brahm's Fourth Symphony. True or not, as she could remember hearing no other kind of music throughout her girlhood, it was no coincidence that other musical preferences—whether jazz, blues, or Oriental—had been acquired in later life and stood second in her affection. Regarding *him* and classical music, since he'd generally tended to avoid it and never volunteered much information about his exposure, she'd surmised that either the latter had been minimal or else he'd had a good dose and hadn't been impressed. That said, his soft spot for *The Firebird* had been as undeniable as—the times she'd dragged him to this or that concert—his instinctive perception of a good performance (*see* Music/Summary/Instruments: Flute and Music/Miscellaneous/*Firebird, The*).

Greek: During their seven days on Thassos, Greek music in one form or another had poured out of every taverna. When, near the end of their stay, the couple began calculating whether they'd taken sufficient snaps and purchased enough presents, it had suddenly occurred to her it would also be lovely to bring home some of what they'd heard. He'd agreed, and they'd immediately gone out and bought a whole fistful of tapes of popular music, which—once back in England—they began to listen to on a regular basis. In fact, unlike gazing at their photos (which, in time, waned), the pair never really put the tapes away and stopped listening altogether. On the contrary, after a time both came to realise that Greek music overall probably meant more to them than any holiday, past or future (*see* Biography/Joint: Greece [Thassos] and Music/Summary).

Jazz: *See* Passions/Miscellaneous: Jazz.

Opera: She had always loved grand opera—with a penchant for the warhorses of the French and Italian repertoires, though her undoubted favourite happened to be a Russian standard, *Boris Goudonov*. He had never been to an opera in his life, and it had been her great (if unrealised) wish during their time together that she should introduce him at some point. Reasons for the failure ranged from tickets for one she knew he'd like (any by Puccini, for example, or similar tunes without too belaboured a plot) always being sold out before she got her act together or (the only instance she *did* get tickets in time) his already being too ill to go. After his death, her opera going had become even more tentative. Floods of quite unstoppable tears at the climax of a performance of *La Traviata* had demonstrated that she was no longer up to watching the soprano die of a lingering illness in the last act and that she'd have to limit herself to those operas where the characters simply killed each other off or the few comic ones that came along from time to time (*see* Passions/Cinema: Tarkovsky, A.).

$\mathcal{P}$

$\mathcal{P}$assions

Summary

During their time together, certain people, things, and institutions had held a sufficiently profound place in the affection of the pair to be labelled "passions." These numbered twenty-four in all, of which the overwhelming majority (eighteen) belonged to him while three were hers and three jointly held. The nature of the passions varied: animals, art, cinema, gardening, history, jazz, religious holidays, America, and Japan composed the list with—interestingly—items in the last two categories belonging to him even though *she* was the native of the former and, of the pair, the traveller to the latter. The great importance of passions to the individual was recognised by them both to the extent that, with one exception, every passion existing in the relationship was instinctively understood as integral a part of its possessor as his or her character or appearance and respected as such (*see* Love/General: Understanding and Passions/America: various).

AMERICA

Cactus: She had unquestioningly associated his passion for different kinds of cactus with his fascination for the American West, since— as far as she was aware—that was their natural home. Though the examples that made up his collection were (in her eyes at least) unusual rather than beautiful, lack of conventional beauty did not stop him from holding the species in tenderer regard than any other indoor or outdoor flora. Indeed, no excursion to a garden centre was ever considered complete until they'd stopped and gazed at its display of little cacti and he'd reminded her yet again that if ever she wanted to buy him a plant as a gift, any of these fellows would do fine. Her own feelings toward cacti were more ambiguous. Prior to meeting him, she'd owned only one, and *its* primary virtue had been an ability to thrive on the sort of erratic care that had either distressed or killed off many other of her houseplants (*see* Garden/Summary and Passions/America: West, American).

West, American: Not unlike bouillabaisse, one's initial sampling of the West had a marked influence on one's later attitude toward it. She, for example, had only once been to a small bit of the West via a business trip to Texas, New Mexico, and Arizona. Though taken to see blooming cacti in an outdoor desert museum at one point (very nice), what she'd ultimately remembered about her western adventure were (a) the inhabitants of each state declaring *their* Mexican food to be the most authentic and insisting she eat gobs of it so that by the time she'd reached her final destination, California, she'd been unspeakably ill; (b) a chronic thirst in Arizona that no amount of liquid could shift; and (c) the initial amusement of the folks in New Mexico (since they'd been experiencing a six-month drought) on seeing the raincoat she'd brought along and then their astonishment when it bucketed down with rain the first night she was there. He, by comparison, had toured through a great deal of the most breathtaking scenery the West had to offer, and at a pace that had fully allowed it to work its magic. When one added to that (a) a childhood spent as an ersatz cowboy, (b) the experience of watching endless Westerns both in the cinema and on telly, and (c) a lack of prejudice about New York City being the centre of the known universe, his abiding passion for the region (as clearly demonstrated by all the photographs, homemade videos, books on the subject, and six of the finest sketches he'd ever done) had seemed preordained (*see* Art/Subjects: Landscapes; Biography/His:

Cowboy; Biography/Hers: New York City; Diet/Exotic: Bouillabaisse; and Passions/America: Cactus).

ART

Bacon, F.: Prior to their relationship, whenever she'd heard the name
Francis Bacon mentioned it had generally been in terms of (a) a
grudging acknowledgement of his talent *or* (b) the grudging ac-
kowledgement immediately followed up with a lament on the
manner in which the talent had manifested itself *or* (c) a downright
refusal to admit he had any talent at all. No one, in her experience,
had ever raved about Bacon's work and called him a genius—at
least no one until she'd met him, though *his* adulation of Bacon was
of an intensity to more than make up for a lifetime of doubting
Thomases. As her own view of Bacon was squarely in *b*, she'd been
fascinated at his enthusiasm and had not only listened eagerly when
he'd extolled the other painter's totally original vision but had
likewise recognised the latter's influence in a great deal of his own
work. That said, nothing was able to bring her to the point of liking
the more extreme examples of Bacon's art (*see* Art/Concepts:
Imitation, Modern art and Passions/Art: Gogh, V. van).

Frink, E.: She hadn't really known about his passion for Elizabeth
Frink until the day they had sat down to plan their trip to Swanage.
Granted, he'd occasionally referred to the sculptress during their
time together and his utter concentration during a television
documentary about her life and work had been noteworthy. But
neither fact had prepared her for (a) his demand that either en route
or on the return trip, they stop at Salisbury *solely* to take in Frink's
The Walking Madonna in its cathedral grounds; b) once there,
indeed devoting more time and attention to the *Madonna* than to the
entire cathedral and its cloisters; and (c) his insistence—when she'd
said she'd like a photo of him—on posing next to the sculpture and
nowhere else. Since he didn't own a biography of Frink, from that

time on she'd looked out for a really good one at every gift-giving occasion—though sadly, she'd been unable to find what she wanted before he'd died (*see* Biography/Joint: Travel and Passions/Art: Matisse, H.).

Giacometti, A.: On her very first visit to his parents' home in Kent, she'd been taken to see a shed chock-full of very early sculptures he had either repudiated entirely, not repudiated but felt he could leave behind, or simply hadn't had room for after he'd moved. Whichever, because of their number and upright position, the sculptures had reminded her of the famous Chinese terracotta warriors except that *his* lot had an unmistakable Giacometti-ish air to them. A later demonstration of this particular passion had occurred during their time in New York when—while walking through a very posh gallery—they'd come upon several examples of the great man's work and he had stood first mesmerised by and then compulsively taking photos of one piece after another. Interestingly, though the bulk of his own sculpture had been as far from Giacometti's style as one could imagine, in the two clay maquettes begun just weeks before his death, his debt to the Swiss sculptor had suddenly and mysteriously re-emerged (*see* Art/Form: Sculpture; Art/Materials: Clay; Biography/His: England; and Biography/Joint: New York City).

Gogh, V. van: Unlike Bacon, van Gogh was an artist for whom she could understand the world's passion. Indeed, while she wouldn't have labelled her own affection for him as such—at least not when compared to her feelings for Redon or Vermeer—she wouldn't have denied it came close. *His* passion for van Gogh, on the other hand, was absolute and was reflected in, among other things, (a) the several books about the painter he owned (as compared to just one for absolutely all other artists); (b) his instant gravitation to the van Goghs no matter what else a museum happened to offer alongside them; and (c) the distinct van Gogh-ish quality of several of his own paintings, an influence probably more pronounced than that of any other painter, Bacon included (*see* Art/Concepts: Imitation; Passions: Bacon, F., Redon, O., Vermeer, J.).

Klee, P.: *See* Biography/Joint: Guggenheim.

Matisse, H.: Somewhat like her mastery of the video camera, his passion for Matisse could not exist apart from the physical objects inspiring it—that is, it tended to erupt only when he stood in front of the actual paintings and at no other time. Thus, unlike other of his "artist" passions, she had few memories of him poring over reproductions of Matisse's paintings or feeling compelled to pay attention to written or televised biographies of the painter. Indeed, Matisse's inclusion at all on the "Passions" list was primarily due to the intensity of his enthusiasm when he *had* expressed it and the accompanying scorn he'd poured upon her at such times for being the only person he could think of who couldn't see what all the fuss was about. More understandably than, say, in the case of Elizabeth Frink, no book about the painter had graced his shelves, though *unlike* Frink, she hadn't been about to go out and hunt one down (*see* Art/Concepts: Modern art; House/Miscellaneous: Appliances and Passions/Art: Frink, E.).

Redon, O.: Odilon Redon ranked as her second favourite artist, coming just behind Vermeer. His oils and pastels had, over the years, actually appeared in a number of her dreams while the mystery of his obscurity rendered him a personal cause célèbre. In that regard, she vividly recalled an experience she'd had while still living in New York. Having raved to a companion about the fabulous Redon pastels they were going to see at the Museum of Modern Art, once they'd arrived she'd found herself unable to locate even one. Instead, there had seemed to be room after room of Picassos—good ones, bad ones, it didn't seem to matter. Though later she'd wondered if the pictures she'd had in mind weren't *actually* at the Met, at the time she'd assumed that to make space for every last button of the Emperor's new clothes her man had been sacrificed, and (unable to locate any other museum officials) had duly vented her fury on the poor souls at the Information Desk. During their time together, she had been delighted to find a book on Redon's lithographs in his collection, though he'd insisted it had been purchased *comme ça* during a trip to Paris. That notwithstanding, not only had he been agreeable to hanging one of her Redon prints in their bedroom in House No. 2, but when a catalogue for a long overdue London exhibition of the artist's work became available in local bookshops, he had (despite its fabulous price) determined to buy it for her for their second anniversary. She had declined his offer saying it would mean much more to her once they'd been to the exhibition itself. In the event, he'd died before either of them could get there; there was no anniversary and the catalogue (now replete with unfortunate associations) had remained unpurchased (*see* Passion/Art: Gogh, V. van and Passions/Cinema: Keaton, B.).

Vermeer, J.: In her eyes, Johannes Vermeer was the alpha and omega of artists: a genius who'd not simply put all his own contemporaries in the shade but—different styles notwithstanding—had never been equalled in the centuries following his death. By the time they'd met, she could lay claim to having seen most of the Vermeers still extant and having read more or less all there was to read about the man and his technique. Given their Klee experience in New York, she'd sorely regretted that they hadn't had the opportunity of viewing even one of Vermeer's paintings together—a regret that deepened when the very year after he'd died, she'd learned of a mammoth exhibition of the artist's work (the greatest cluster of his paintings gathered in a single location since the seventeenth century) coming to the Hague. That said, believing he wouldn't have wanted her to miss such an opportunity, she'd made a point of journeying to Holland to see it (*see* Biography/Joint: Guggenheim and Passions/Art: Redon, O.).

Wood: Though he'd never actually said so while they were together, his passion for wood had to have been profound. As a carpenter he'd earned his living by it and as a sculptor not merely used it as his premier material but had understood its nature to the point of apparently being able to transcend it by fashioning shapes and surfaces that looked as if they might as easily have been poured from a molten substance. Little wonder then that among a pile of magazines, the single coffee-table *book* displayed first by him and later by them in House No. 2 had been an enormous, elegant, and patently expensive tome called *Wood* (in her eyes, a printed allegory of himself) (*see* Art/Form: Sculpture; Art/Materials: Wood and Work/His: Carpentry, Joinery).

CINEMA

Cameras: Like the unexpected drum kit, she'd only become aware of the number of cine cameras, projectors, and related gadgets in his possession at the time of their move to House No. 2. As they'd unearthed one thing after another, the collection had spread out on the floor before them like a mini-museum suddenly sprung to life. For pure variety, it seemed to rival his records and tapes, except that this lot didn't come with labels, and his offhand identifications were too quick for her to fix in her mind what was what or how old it might be. Ultimately, it had been enough to understand that (a) his love of the cinema had extended even to its equipment, (b) over the years, he had tried out most of what he owned, while (c) the remainder he'd kept either for sentimental reasons or—again like his record and tapes—for the sake of historical completeness (*see* Music/Instruments: Drum kits; Music/Miscellaneous: Sound production; and Music/Musicians: Beiderbecke, B.).

Cinema: His passion for all aspects of the cinema had been a major fact of their lives. The conventional bit of that passion—a fascination with films, actors, and directors—had mirrored her own, though more intense and better informed. His experiences as a filmmaker, however, were something else again. She couldn't recall ever before knowing someone whose cinema involvement had gone beyond endless attitudinising—but his *had* done. Even as a young lad, he'd messed about with cameras and such, as countless reels of organised, if not scripted, silent films, speeded-up, backwards, or time-elapsed shots all testified to. As a grown man, he had attended a film workshop, and with a fellow attendee later collaborated on a number of short films and film fragments—scripts jointly written by the pair, the friend acting as director and he as cinematographer. Indeed, the stunning colour photography in one of these collaborations—a documentary about a local beauty spot—had left her wondering how any one man could be quite so multi-talented. That said, fate (in the guise of one commercial disappointment after another) had decreed that ultimately neither man was to make filmmaking his career (*see* Abilities/Summary/Do-It-Yourself, Photography; Character: Humourousness; and Work/His: Animation).

Keaton, B.: Privately, she'd always suspected that his passion for Buster Keaton was not unlike her own for Odilon Redon. Each believed his or her particular hero to be inexplicably underrated in comparison to more famous peers and had made that opinion known. In his case, the latter had been effected not via public temper tantrums (they weren't in his character) but through (a) the ownership of a video as well as a book about Keaton's life and work—the single example (bar a telly programme he'd once taped re Andrei Tarkovsky) of the former in his possession and (b) the natural expectation, after a joint viewing of the above-mentioned video, that she, too, could not help but be convinced of Keaton's greatness. In fact, her post-video attitude had stayed pretty much the same as the pre-video one: Keaton was all right, but she far and away preferred Charlie Chaplin—though nothing in the world would have prompted her to tell him so (*see* Character: Diffidence, Self-effacement; Love/General: Openness; Passions/Art: Redon; O.; and Passions/Cinema: Tarkovsky, A.).

Tarkovsky, A.: Of the couple's three shared passions, Andrei Tarkovsky is perhaps the most interesting. She never learned how *he* had come to revere the great Russian director—he hadn't bothered to explain but rather treated Tarkovsky's genius as a fact of nature, not requiring comment. No doubt all he knew about the technical side of filmmaking had contributed, but such knowledge wasn't necessary to come under the spell. In the pre-him years, she'd known an individual whose (non-technical) passion had been of a calibre to prompt him to travel to London from the south of England during a monumental snowstorm simply not to miss a Tarkovsky festival. Her own passion for the Russian, by comparison, had begun with a pronounced resistance . . . a feeling that his films were quirky and mannered. And then she'd seen *Andrei Rublev* and done a complete *volte face.* Never before had she come in contact with a film that (a) switched from black and white to colour, let alone with such effect, (b) gave the viewer the uncanny feeling of what it must have been like to live during a remote period in the past, and (c) rendered every single character—no matter how unimportant— wholly believable. Indeed, the moment in the film when a Tartar warrior is unexpectedly nonplussed by the actions of an idiot peasant girl and momentarily wavers in his machismo ranked, in her mind, as *the* most authentic and affecting in all cinema. Soon after seeing the film, she'd attended a performance of *Boris Goudonov.* A "Boris" aficionado, she had been to more versions of the opera than she cared to remember and while always enthralled by the music and spectacle, had generally suffered the acting as the price one paid for them. But this particular performance happened to have been directed by Tarkovsky, and once again she was completely bowled over. For the first time, the dramatic situation became equal to the music. In fact, had Boris never sung a single note, she still would have been transfixed by his plight. After *that* experience, she was hooked. She made a point of again looking at all the films she'd previously dismissed and decided she must have been mad: each one was more wonderful than the next. Thus was the ground well prepared for the joint Tarkovsky worship that began when the pair met and that lasted, without interruption, throughout the relationship (*see* Music/Types: Opera; Passions/Art: Klee, P.; and Passions/Cinema: Tati, J.).

Tati, J.: Unlike Tarkovsky, one's passion for Jacques Tati could never be thought of as achievable; one either took to him or not, full stop. As regards the two of them, each had independently fallen in love with Tati's effortless charm and humour, and once together had been quite happy to watch one or another of the films on video—invariably commenting to each other how clever this or that part happened to be and chuckling throughout, though each had seen whatever film it might be countless times before (*see* Passions/Cinema: Tarkovsky, A.).

HOLIDAYS

Christmas: Having had the opportunity of sharing two Christmases with him, she'd felt an intense curiosity about the genesis of his passion for the season. The single *legitimate* reason for all the fuss (religion) didn't seem to apply and even Christmas as a license to indulge could not explain the labour he was prepared to expend. That labour officially began with designing and producing his own Christmas cards, admittedly no big deal for an artist though both did take time. He'd then agonise over his card list—who was to get a card, who not, and (horror of horrors) would he manage to get a card to X in time because X (who *hadn't* been on his list) had sent him one. Next came digging out a collection of the most appalling tinsel she'd ever laid eyes on and proceeding to festoon every inch of the house with it until the whole place looked like some demented grotto designed by the Seven Dwarfs. This was quickly followed by the gift worry phase—a variation of card worry in that while the gifts were fewer in number, their acquisition required consultation and the bother of somehow finding them. Then almost before one knew it was time for the Christmas party phase—a Herculean labour he'd taken on for himself every year and which his friends and acquaintances had come to expect. After that was Christmas Day—of the whole rigmarole perhaps the most mystifying to her since the amount of time preparing the Christmas dinner and cleaning up after it far exceeded the amount of time opening up one's gifts or doing anything else she would have called enjoyable. Finally, New Year's Eve would loom on the horizon, though as he'd already done his entertaining, *that* didn't involve much beyond (a) getting somewhere else, (b) enjoying oneself for the minimum hours the honour of New Year's Eve demanded, and (c) getting back again. And that, thank God, was it. How he—or anyone really—could actually look forward to it all was beyond her. But then, as he'd repeatedly point out, she hadn't experienced his childhood Christmases: mother year in year out feasting what had seemed like the 5,000; the amateur entertainments organised by himself; the excitement over one's presents and having family and friends around. A twenty-minute eggnog tipple with the only Christians living in one's building, and unsuccessfully nagging one's parents for a "Hanukkah bush" just wasn't the same. That notwithstanding (and to her shame), Christmas was to prove the one passion of his she'd felt driven to tamper with, and thus it happened that for their second festive season together, not only were decorations confined to a tasteful arrangement around the tree, but Christmas dinner was eaten in a restaurant. Frankly, had he lived she'd fully planned to talk him into Christmas abroad—ideally in a Moslem country (*see* Abilities: Baking; Beliefs: God, Religion; Biography/ Joint: New Year's Eves; Cookery/Specialties/Hers: Vegetarian cassoulet; Cookery/Specialties/His: various; Diet/Summary/Compulsive/Harmful: Coffee; Love/General: Sentimentality, Understanding; and Passions/Summary).

Easter: Though in no way approaching Christmas mania, there was little doubt that his affection for Easter was of an order to crank him into activity mode. The giving, receiving, and vigorous consumption of chocolate Easter eggs of all sizes; arranging some sort of tea *chez eux;* perhaps painting real eggs and/or planting jelly beans throughout the garden for guests with small children and the purchase of cards, flowers, and gifts for one's nearest and dearest were all standard. While logic told her the whole thing was probably as much a routine as Christmas, it couldn't quite explain why she didn't mind. Perhaps it was because Easter took less time and generally happened in nicer weather than Christmas. Or that they could get through it without house decorations. Or that she had a holiday ritual totally independent of him in the form of a standing Easter Sunday luncheon invitation from close friends. Or all of the above (*see* Passions/Holidays: Christmas).

JAPAN

Sumo wrestling: His passion for sumo wrestling had been overwhelming. Not merely a devotee of the competitions shown on British telly, he'd also attended its first demonstration in London and (had he possessed the money) undoubtedly would have travelled to Japan to experience sumo in its original setting. Beyond all of that, however, he'd obsessed over sumo wrestlers as a subject for his art. Hectares of huge, scantily clad bodies either in the formal poses prior to a bout or tumbling every which way—buttocks to the forefront was a favourite—had filled painting after painting, as well as provided the subject for jointed wooden puppets ranging in size from modest to larger than life. She *supposed* she could understand what it was all about. She, too, had watched the sumo matches on telly and been fascinated at the enormous expanses of flesh (particularly in a country of generally slight people) and the marked differences to Western-style wrestling. That said, no amount of fascination would ever have convinced her that the paintings and puppets weren't gross (*see* Art/Summary).

Sushi: Considering how he'd always refused to purchase raw shrimp from the fishmonger or supermarket, his passion for sushi had been unexpected. Its disclosure dated back to an evening in New York when they'd first gone for Japanese food with her favourite cousin— an addict in her own right. To say his excitement (at the cousin's announcement that they were sitting in one of the best sushi restaurants in the neighbourhood) had been palpable would be an understatement; *both* of them had given her the impression of two junkies suddenly admitted into crack heaven. A discussion in hushed tones about the different kinds of sushi on the menu ended with the pair ordering two deluxe platters. Even more extraordinary—once the food had arrived—were the moments when one of them would pause while eating to get his breath and the other would volunteer to have whatever was still on their plate. Her own attitude to sushi had been immutably fixed during a visit to Japan years earlier, when friends had taken her to *their* top sushi restaurant, and started the meal with something having the consistency of a rubber band. Fifteen minutes of concentrated chewing and all the saliva she could muster hadn't been able to break it down, and getting a bit desperate (she wasn't about to insult her friends by spitting it out), she'd *finally* managed to swallow the beastly thing only on a tidal wave of sake. Consequent drunkenness had pretty much blurred the memory of the remainder of the meal. Perhaps what followed had been tasty—perhaps not. All she could remember was that the rubber band was to stick in her mind as much as it had done in her mouth, causing her to pass on sushi ever thereafter (*see* Biography/Joint: New York City; Diet/Healthful: Shrimp; and Passions/Summary).

MISCELLANEOUS

Animals: *See* Garden/Areas: Wildlife; Garden/Inhabitants: various; and Pets/Summary: Cats.

Garden: *See* Abilities: various; Attitudes: Ecology; Biography/His: England; Character: Heroism; Garden/Summary/Areas: Flowers, Pond; and House/Summary.

History: Throughout her girlhood, history had been synonymous with England—a filmed version of Queen Elizabeth's coronation (shown in the cinema) and, some time later, probably one of the first BBC series sold to American television (called *An Age of Kings* and depicting all of Shakespeare's English historical plays) had effected the introduction. After that, all of her history came via school, where—happily—the deadly presentation had not extinguished her interest. On the contrary—at some point in her teens, England had been replaced by a universal fascination with the subject. Once a devotee, she'd quickly become fussy about the kind of history she'd bother with (this being, for the most part, social history with a healthy dose of those facts hacked out of "standard" versions). Perhaps what had always struck her, even more than what they neglected to teach one, was the conceit of her own time—how it was simply taken for granted that everything from determining pregnancy through urinalysis to genocide to vegetarianism had naturally begun during *these* hundred years (*see* Biography/Hers: England and Work/Summary/Hers: various).

Jazz: Jazz had been his equivalent of her classical music: the reigning sound passion; the music against which all others—no matter how much enjoyed—would always come second. Like so many other of his passions, the involvement hadn't been passive. He'd (a) played the drums (in his youth in a jazz band and in later years for himself), (b) messed around with learning the trombone and just before he died, the double bass, and (c) possessed a mini-library of books, discs, tapes, and CDs not to mention several first-class drum kits. That said, *unlike* his other passions (e.g., sumo; the American West), his passion for jazz had not seemed to influence his art. Even photographs of his beloved Chet Baker (prominently displayed in his studio in their country house) had not, as far as she could see, spawned so much as a sketch of the musician—or at least anything he'd kept. Indeed, if he'd referred at all to the pics, it had been as a visual aid to his occasional narratives of Baker's life. His taste in jazz had run to modern, and she (who liked trad) had found him implacable about not attending trad gigs. All the same, it was generally trad she'd heard him play at home—for which she'd been sincerely, if silently, thankful (*see* Love/General: Openness; Music/Summary/Instruments: Drum kit; Music/Miscellaneous: *Firebird, The,* Sound production; Music/Musicians: various; Music/Types: Classical; and Passions/America: West, American; and Passions/Miscellaneous: Jazz).

$\mathcal{P}$*ets*

Summary

If he was anything to judge by, a childhood in the country meant animals. During their time together, he'd told her of the cats, dogs, and more exotic species (at least exotic to her) such as goats, chickens, and ponies that had been around while he was growing up. She, by contrast, could count her animal contact on two fingers. The first had been when (as a very small girl) she'd refused to accept her parents' statement that animals weren't allowed in their building and nagged and nagged until they'd finally bought her three itsy-bitsy turtles. These she'd named Myrtle, Sam, and Irving and loved and tended until the fateful day when setting them on the edge of the bathroom sink to clean their bowl, all three had hopped into the toilet and immediately swum off to join the reptile population of the New York City sewer system. Her second encounter had been in adulthood on the occasion of an extended visit home sometime after her mother's second marriage. Her new stepbrother (in a noble attempt to replace a much loved pet chihuahua of his father's who'd been killed while at the same time *not* alarm her mother who would have died rather than own a quadruped) had hit upon a bird as the answer and given their parents a beautiful white canary (called Stanley). Though her stepfather had declared that *he* would look after Stanley, by the time she'd arrived, responsibility for the canary had somehow passed to her mother. It was not a happy arrangement. Even allowing that woman and bird had a bond in their common love of Mozart (the latter singing his little heart out whenever anything of Mozart's played on the radio or cassette), a shared subscription to the New York Philharmonic could not have disguised their mutual terror. Attempts to change Stanley's seed or water generally left the canary practically falling off his perch from dread and Mother with a case of the shakes. Soon things had got so bad that the distinctive grey fringe over Stanley's eyes began to go white and—not to be outdone—Mother claimed she was developing eczema. At this point, her stepfather had had to take action though, inexplicably, it wasn't to keep his original pledge. Instead, he decided to place Stanley with an aviary-owning acquaintance—and that had ended that. Privately, she'd shared her mother's relief at the canary's departure and in general was quite prepared to leave pets to other people. That is, until she met him and "other people" became her cohabitant (*see* Biography/His: England; Garden/Areas: Wildlife; Garden/Inhabitants: various; and Pets: Cats).

Cats: There could be no question that cats had ranked among his greatest passions. With little or no provocation, he could (and often had) launched into veritable paeans about them while her eyes would glaze over. She hated cats. Having inherited her mother's dislike of all animals (with the possible exception of itsy-bitsy turtles), cats had always come near the top of the list. Her reaction upon finding *two* of them the first time she'd gone to his home can only be imagined though, it must be said, one hadn't actually belonged to him and had exited the scene too quickly to be a problem. The remaining cat, however (one Fluffy by name), had more than made up for that departure as the following survey of attitudes amply demonstrates. *1. Appearance: He:* Fluffy was nothing less than a gorgeous white confection with alluring little touches of black. *She:* Fluffy had to be the only cat she'd ever seen with chronically rheumy eyes, as if he were always on the point of but never quite managing to recover from a cold. *He:* Like all cats, Fluffy kept himself immaculately clean. *She:* Nothing could be considered clean that was covered with a coat of its own saliva. *2. Behaviour: He:* If Fluffy invariably chose her parents' £5,000 Astrakhan carpet on which to disgorge some badly digested victim, well—it was unfortunate but cats were like that. Anyway, he didn't do it often. *She:* He made a specialty of it. And for utterly repulsive behaviour, *that* little trick surpassed even the nastiness of slugs, and slugs required neither slug food nor expensive visits to the vet. *He:* Fluffy only wanted to be her friend. *She:* Fluffy was crazed with jealousy as was more than testified to by (a) his jumping up and down and generally throwing a tantrum whenever they kissed until they'd stop kissing; she'd say: "Go on, kiss the cat" and he did, and (b) thinking he had a right to watch them make love (fat chance) and when discovering he hadn't, hurling himself against the bedroom door for a solid fifteen minutes *every single time. He:* Everyone who visited their home fell in love with Fluffy. *She:* Everyone didn't have much choice given that Fluffy would launch into a standard hysterical attention-getting routine so that just to get intelligent conversation going again, a lap had to be offered for him to claw his way into position upon. *3. Cleverness: He:* Cats were infinitely cleverer than dogs. *She:* If Fluffy was clever, she wondered what he classed as stupid. Seven trillion admonitions about (a) *not* sleeping on their dining table or any other surface in the kitchen, (b) *not* treating his jumpers as a kitty litter, (c) bloody staying out of their bedroom, and (d) leaving her alone **because she didn't like him** hadn't, during their time together, registered in Fluffy's little brain. *4.*

Devotion: He: Fluffy loved him as much as he loved Fluffy. *She:* As long as he was in Fluffy's range of vision, maybe. Personally, she didn't regard (a) leaving the neighbours he'd been installed with and trotting off to the next county, (b) making himself at home with the first bunch who happened to feed him, and (c) acting huffy at being taken from the latter—all because his master had had the cheek to go on holiday—love. And yet with all of that, she couldn't deny that every time Fluffy was hoisted onto his hind legs for a cavort to Duke Ellington or fell asleep with his head twisted upside down or burrowed under paper and/or hid himself in cardboard boxes, she could *almost* understand the reasons for his addiction. Regrettably, she'd never told him this or once thought to reassure him that, bombast aside, he needn't be concerned; it was not in her to neglect a living creature. Indeed, once on her own she'd felt sorry about not caring enough for Fluffy to be prepared to do anything but feed him, and through a mutual friend, had soon arranged for him to be looked after by someone more suitable (*see* Garden/Inhabitants: Frogs, Slugs; House/Miscellaneous: Chores; Music/Musicians: Ellington, D.; Pets: Dogs; and Sex: various).

Dogs: In her eyes, dogs had it over cats. Get the right breed and they were handsome, loyal, bright, and unashamedly affectionate. True, she would never have owned or even picked one up, but petting, scratching, and cooing over the little sweeties were quite in order. Had she ever been pressed to justify this preference, she could have pointed to no feline equivalent of Lassie or Rin Tin Tin and *dogs* traditionally being thought of as man's best friend. Of course, neither fact would have impressed him. Contrary evidence never did count to a devotee, and both in the pre- and post-him years, she'd heard enough dyed-in-the-fur cat lovers (admittedly, with occasional justification) dismiss dogs as smelly, dirty, sickeningly dependent, and lacking personality. Fair enough. Two sides of the coin was part of what gave the coin its value. Looking back on it, she would have said it had been *less* his love of cats per se that she'd resented than that the accompanying dog contempt had been based on a double standard in animal behaviour (as in cat-regurgitated creatures at one's feet were a regrettable foible whereas *one* soppy, smelly dog was apparently enough to put the species beyond the pale). And what of his chummy behaviour with his parents' dog every time they visited? In her eyes, it had smacked more of hypocrisy than diplomacy. Not that she'd expected him to attack the creature, but—given his oft-repeated vituperation—he could have ignored it, as she'd always sought to ignore Fluffy. During their time together, repeated references to the contradictions in both his reasoning and behaviour had made little difference; he'd politely listen and offer no response. No doubt he believed that given her general attitude toward *and* woeful inexperience with all animals, she was hardly in a position to comment let alone pass judgment (*see* Love/General: Openness and Pets/Summary: Dogs).

S

Self-Image

Summary

Emergence from their respective psychic shells was probably the one significant image change for the couple during their time together. Otherwise, the largely destructive assessments each brought to the relationship had carried on—resistant alike to affection, the contentment that affection generated, and (on her part, at least) repeated efforts toward modification. In this regard, she'd been unable to see that (a) her crusade to ameliorate his self-image probably had as much to do with the top end of her *own* self-image (a complicated business involving alternating fantasies of worthlessness and omnipotence) as any manifestation of love and that (b) like it or not, *no* amount of acting as his champion was going to disperse feelings of inferiority that reached right down to the core of his being. For his part, with the single exception of now and then tut-tutting her over-critical views of her appearance, he'd not been inclined to do the same. Even had it been in his character to try, the sliding scale on which she operated would have made the task daunting if not altogether impossible (*see* Abilities/Summary; Biography/His: School; Character: Diffidence, Intelligence, Self-effacement; Love/General: Emergence; Self-image/ Contributing to: Age; and Work/Summary).

CONTRIBUTING TO

Age: While the pair was no longer young, at no point during their time together did age appear to hurt their respective self-images.

Both carried their years well and, not having known one another as younger individuals, had not witnessed processes of physical deterioration. On the contrary, not only had each been attracted to and fallen in love with the other in middle age, but the various benefits of a relationship at this time of life—though not *specifically* touching on appearance—had still exerted a salutary effect on how each saw himself in relation to the world (*see* Love/Summary/ General: Monogamy; and Self-image/Contributing to: various).

Body: *See* Biography/His: Leanness; Character: Youthfulness; Illness/ Summary/Last (His)/Symptoms: Weight loss; Love/General: Monogamy; and Love/Specific: Caressing.

Dress: Both of them had had very definite ideas about their apparel. She was generally conservative in taste and reluctant to upgrade her wardrobe—such behaviour being the sad but perhaps inevitable result of never being allowed to choose her own clothes because her mother had envied her figure and dressed vicariously through her— whereas he'd liked to dress unconventionally (bright red shoes and a matching red belt, for example, being standard accessories for any and all of his shirts and trousers if he felt in the mood). She'd admired him for his flamboyance but felt unable to imitate it, and he (though he had likely felt she didn't do herself justice) often complimented her on her appearance. The above notwithstanding, at times each one had expressed pet peeves concerning some aspect of the other's dress. The worst of these, specifically, her fanatical detestation of cowboy boots, had ultimately compelled him to hang up the pair he'd owned—though she knew the boots had meant more to him than the rest of his shoes put together. Fortunately for the relationship, all *other* peeves (such as how he hated her in beige and how she just knew that tight jeans and trousers were the opposite of flattering to him) were stoically listened to and then ignored (*see* Illness/Last [His]/Experiences: Stoma and Love/ Summary; Self-image/Summary: Hats, Neckties).

Exercise: Exercise represents an interesting dichotomy in the self-images of the pair. With the exception of weight lifting, he hadn't perceived exercise as something "one did" beyond ordinary life activities, which—if one was as naturally active as he—anyway kept one trim. She, by contrast, had (a) never been particularly active in the first place, (b) ignored exercise-cum-exercise for as long as she could get away with it, and (c) on reaching the age when that was no longer possible, she'd taken it up with all the enthusiasm of a convert, ranking it only behind penicillin in the blessing stakes (*see* Attitudes: Health maintenance; Character: Laziness; Love/General: Monogamy; and Self-image: Muscle).

Face: Shortly after they'd begun dating, he'd called on the woman who'd introduced them and declared: "Your friend must like short, ugly men." Whether (a) not being tall rendered a man ugly by definition or (b) he had genuinely thought he had an unpleasant face, there can be no question that this particular area had been a sticky one for him. Her opinion of her own face hadn't been quite so punitive. Though possessing neither the pronounced cheekbones nor Roman nose that accounted for her own ideal of facial beauty (she probably had to be the one Jewess alive who'd wished her nose were *bigger*), on good days she nevertheless felt she could be reasonably attractive. Predictably, neither self-image had been reflected in the loving eyes of the one whose face it wasn't, and each had thought the other mad for not realising how totally handsome/beautiful he or she happened to be (*see* Biography/Hers: Jew and Biography/Joint: Spectacles).

Hats: A pronounced fondness for hats had been a feature of his wardrobe. One of his most treasured purchases during their time in New York had been a leather baseball cap that, for some reason, the vendor had been willing to let go at cost. He'd lived in that cap once they'd got back to England—particularly when it rained. But lots of males in England wore baseball caps of one sort or another. What had intrigued her far more—as much for the use he'd put it to as for itself—was his fabulous beige suede Borsalino, with a thick band of what looked to her like partridge feathers edging the crown. Worn at the appropriate rakish angle, the Borsalino had contributed as much to the jaunty self he liked to effect now and then as bopping around to Duke Ellington. Indeed, the two had often gone together. As for her and hats, since ninety-five percent of them ruined the coiffure she considered vital to *her* public self, they'd become a no-no years back (*see* Attitudes: Rain; Biography/Joint: New York City; Music/Musicians: Ellington, D.; and Self-image: Dress).

Learning: His rabid belief in his inability to learn was never discussed between the two during their time together. On the one hand, she'd felt this was a pity, since she'd have been only too happy to provide a list of the accomplishments—from art to carpentry to photography to playing various musical instruments—that blatantly gave it the lie. On the other hand, in her heart of hearts she knew that all the lists in the world could not disassociate the concept of learning, that is, being taught, from the painful experiences he'd undergone at school. Indeed, as he'd showed equally little interest in all references to the large chunk of the world beyond *her* comprehension, she'd had to conclude the entire topic was verboten (*see* Abilities: various; Biography/His: School; Character: Intelligence; and Music: various).

Literacy: Relinquishment of all letter writing to her and repeated comments about how slowly he read had led her to believe that he did not rate his own literacy very highly. In her opinion, the grounds for such a judgment—difficulties with spelling and his ubiquitous experiences as a schoolboy—were singularly insufficient. During their time together, not only had neither circumstance ever prevented him from reading and offering insightful comments about her work, but in the pre-her years he had (among other projects she was less familiar with) written several children's stories and a fascinating stream-of-conscious fragment about the destruction of his home during the London blitz (this last possibly intended as an explanatory note to his coloured pencil depictions of V-2 rockets) (*see* Abilities: Letter-writing, Spelling; Art/Subjects: Rockets; Biography/His: Rockets, School; and Work/Hers: various).

Menopause: Due in equal part to a happy acceptance of the aging process stemming from her belief in multiple lives and an acknowledgement that to non-maternal types like herself, fundamentally the process had to be a *boon,* the onset of menopause had held no angst. The time she'd missed several periods in a row, for example, learning it was the climacteric and not an unwanted pregnancy, had been a cause for celebration for them both. Likewise after his death—the start of hot flushes had stuck in her mind mainly due to her wrongly attributing it at first to a fault in the central heating system. Soon, however, she was not only to learn in which heating system the problem *actually* lay but how to make it go away through the daily ingestion of oil of evening primrose (*see* Attitudes: Children; Beliefs: Reincarnation; House/Challenges: Heating; and Work/His: Book illustration).

Muscle: Whether to atone for the terrible sin of not being tall—or some other self-perceived unattractiveness—from adolescence he had been a body-building aficionado. Though not a fan of muscular men as a rule, she readily admitted that in his case it hadn't been a bad idea. Indeed, after his death she'd come to realise that her attraction to what she'd initially perceived simply as his leanness had in fact also included admiration of well-developed arms, chest, and legs and, later on, his considerable strength (as in the installation of her magnificent desk). While during their time together he'd used his store of body-building equipment rarely (and then only to keep fit), it was obvious to her how important a good physique counted to his self-esteem and her heart broke to think what horrors were visited on that esteem when cancer began to ravage his body (*see*

Attitudes: Health maintenance; Biography/His: Leanness; House/
Miscellaneous: Desk; Illness/Chronic: Back pain; Illness/Last [His]/
Symptoms: Weight loss; and Love/Specific: Caressing).

Neckties: Along with (the approved) red belt and shoes and
(disapproved) cowboy boots, his flamboyance in dress seemed to
express itself through neckties (though in her opinion, some of them
left flamboyance behind and waded out toward ghastliness). Indeed,
during a necktie acquisition excursion around the time of her
mother's funeral (when he'd been overcome by the $1.00-each price
on a fistful of particular horrors), no amount of her explaining that
the reason they were so cheap was because they verged on the
psychedelic could convince him this wasn't the buy of the century.
All she could do to stop him from actually *wearing* one of them on
the sad day was have him choose from a small selection she'd
requested from a friend—a manoeuvre he'd acquiesced to only
because he'd believed that just this once, her woeful conservatism
was matched by the occasion (*see* Biography/Joint: New York City
and Self-image: Dress, Hats).

Sex

Summary

The couple's attitudes toward beginning a physical relationship had
not been in synch. She had fancied him from the first, very soon felt
the attraction turn to love, and concluded that in the circumstances,
three weeks were stretching it as a platonic period. He, on the other
hand, while indicating his own affection via repeated notes of appreciation and declaring that for the first time with a woman he could utterly be himself, apparently hadn't heard of the three-week rule and
remained a perfect gentleman. This state of affairs (or non-affairs) had
continued until she'd decided that if they weren't to enter their twi-

light years as pals, something had to be done—and one Sunday as they strolled down the street, she'd put her arm through his and announced that they should spend the following weekend together. To defuse the moment, she'd then joked about making him feel better than an expensive masseur he'd raved about *and* being free of charge. He'd seemed a bit stunned, but happy, to accept her proposition. Later they kissed because they thought they should. Though both sensed good things to come, the four days until Friday were a trial. Each had been celibate for many years, and he was obviously shy. In a flurry of nerves, she rang midweek to inform him that the only two things she was really any good at were writing and sex. She'd intended the call as a gesture of intimacy but then wondered if she hadn't lost her mind. Surely that was the *last* bit of information one volunteered in such a situation. Cursing herself every moment, she spent the rest of the day waiting for him to ring back and call the weekend off. But no—his only reaction was to send her a vast bouquet of red roses the following day (he later told her she'd given him a twenty-four-hour erection). Finally the weekend arrived, and the rightness she'd intuited from that single embrace in no way prepared her for what followed: a solid two days in bed in a paroxysm of bliss. Afterward, she was to blush at having boasted of *her* prowess (*see* Biography/Joint: Courtship; Love/General: Sentimentality; Love/Specific: Caressing, Showers, joint, and Sex/Considerations: various).

CONSIDERATIONS

Birth control: In the pre-him years, she had never known a partner who'd liked using a condom. As it turned out that he wouldn't, either, she was grateful that during those years (in the days before "safe sex") she had decided not to rely on them but rather take her own precautions against becoming pregnant. As all and sundry birth control pills had made her ill (not to mention that a medicine she would soon be required to take for life rendered them ineffective anyway), she'd therefore settled on the diaphragm as her preferred method of contraception (*see* Attitudes: Children; Illness/Chronic: Epilepsy; Sex/Considerations: Diaphragm; Sex/Realities: Erections).

Celibacy, previous: The pair represent a good example of both the advantages and disadvantages of long-term celibacy when commencing a new sexual relationship. On the plus side were a number of (admittedly cavalier) assumptions such as (a) AIDS not being a concern, (b) celibacy meaning choosiness, with the corollaries that (c) the new lover was special and therefore (d) the act itself had a good chance of being more meaningful than either a simple release or a kind of Olympic event. On the minus side, one might well include worry about being copacetic in one's sexual tastes and capacities and the likelihood of initial nasty side effects such as cystitis (her) and sore elbows (him) (*see* Biography/Summary and Sex/Summary).

Dependence, physical: While the pair were together long enough for their lovemaking to calm down a bit from its initial flights of fantasy and marathon duration, the time *wasn't* sufficient for a single, unchanging routine to emerge. Thus, mutual physical dependence on the act—particularly as they became increasingly attuned to each other—actually grew and had not plateaued by the time he became terminally ill. Moreover, though his cancer would ultimately put an end to their physical relations, it did not appear to affect his libido so that right up to some weeks before his death, he would repeatedly state how sensitive his penis felt and then bewail the passing of their sex life (*see* Illness/Last [His]/Experiences: Nursing home; Sex/Considerations: Satiety; Sex/Realities: Intercourse, Positions).

Diaphragm: Having concluded in the pre-him years that the diaphragm was appropriate as a birth-control measure, not unnaturally she had assumed that being fitted for one would be a straightforward business. It hadn't. Of the two doctors she'd tried while in New York, the first had been her mother's gynecologist. She was an eminent woman in the field, but over the years she had grown to distrust men and bluntly refused to prescribe *any* contraception to a single woman until she'd heard the name of the lover and if he was amenable to marriage. Doctor No. 2 had been a man who, while not hating women, had too many of them as patients to give her more than thirty seconds of his time and the following user instructions: "Stick it in as far as it can go, and forget about it." No mention was made of anything like covering the cervix, a fact that was brought home to her years later in England when she became pregnant and had to have an abortion. Indeed, the gynecologist at her local family planning clinic couldn't help observing that even had the instructions been correct, the diaphragm *itself* was unsuitable given the peculiar way she was built, so that all in all it was a mystery how she hadn't conceived before. The former quickly added, however, that they could sort something out, and to this end had—like some old-fashioned con man revealing a whole jacketful of watches—flung open an enormous triptych of what appeared to be every cap ever designed and, after a bit more feeling around, correctly fitted her (*see* Sex/Considerations: Birth control and Sex/Involving: Vagina).

Egyptian dance: About a year or so before they'd met, she had taken a series of Egyptian dance classes. The classes had been held in a mirrorless church hall, and one viewing of a videotape of their first public performance had been sufficient to put the kibosh on (a) her vision of herself as a sort of Middle Eastern nautch girl and (b) her participation. Vanity notwithstanding, though, she couldn't deny that the classes *had* improved her pelvic control to the extent that she wondered about what it might be like to exercise it other than on the dance floor. Meeting him had given her the opportunity, and to her delight she found she had the ability to internally squeeze his penis while they were making love. He had hardly been less delighted. Indeed, the first time they went to bed, he'd announced that either she or it—she hadn't been too sure of the pronoun—was the answer to every man's dream (*see* Sex/Considerations: Taste and Sex/Involving Penis).

False alarm: *See* Attitudes: Children and Self-image/Contributing to: Menopause.

Inhibition, lack of: In her experience in the pre-him years, getting over virginity was the big obstacle. Once that occurred, inhibitions had seemed beside the point, and she'd liked to think of herself as at least as adventurous as whoever her partner happened to be. On his side, he'd been too discreet to discuss his previous sexual experiences and for once in her life she'd had the sense not to pry. It was therefore, a distinct surprise—given what an utterly sensual and thorough lover he was—to hear him solemnly vow that never before had he been so uninhibited with a woman. She could only imagine— were it really so and not merely some tactful compliment—that sexually speaking, he had to have spent his life as the human equivalent of a thoroughbred racehorse hitched to a series of milk carts (*see* Love/General: Openness; and Love/Specific: Caressing).

Menstruation: During the pre-him years, the old saw about avoiding sex during one's period because men feared blood on their penises had seemed to be so: Partners *had* generally been reluctant when she was menstruating. She had always felt this was really too bad, but a fact of life—like catarrh. And then she'd met him; they'd begun sleeping together and that time of the month had rolled around. She'd informed him and he'd said, "So?" Surprised, she'd asked if he didn't mind, and he'd responded "No, why?" and she'd explained. To which he'd replied that not only, as it happened, did blood on that particular spot not bother him, but *surely* she didn't imagine anything so silly forcing them into abstinence six days out of every month. At which point she'd answered no, it *was* unimaginable, and that had been that (*see* Biography/Hers: Menstruation and Love/General: Discovery).

Odour: During their time together, he'd repeatedly mentioned that the most skillfully crafted scent could not equal a woman's natural emanations *provided* of course that the proclivities of the smeller happened to match the offerings of the smellee. Of all the happy discoveries she made while living with him, that such a match existed between *them* stood in high relief so that during sex she soon came to expect (a) at least one passionate declaration by him re the intoxicating nature of her odour, (b) repeated inhalations of her nether parts much as if they were a tray of just-baked cookies, and (c) statements of regret that lifelong allergies had rendered her *own* sense of smell close to nonfunctional—though *which* fabulous odour (his, hers, or both) she was missing out on she never did determine (*see* Illness/Chronic: Allergy; Love/General: Discovery; and Sex/Considerations Taste).

Pleasure: During their time together, the intense sexual pleasure the couple was able to achieve was in direct proportion to the intensity of their affection. Personally, she'd always thought that what went under the name of lovemaking was often no more than "likemaking"—if that—though over the years she'd tended to keep this observation to herself since it sounded pretentious not to mention old-fashioned, and only once before (with the first man who'd died) had she been in a situation where it had applied. Her surprise, therefore, when out of the blue *he* declared that without the feelings they had for each other, their lovemaking could never be as sublime, had been intense. Along with his lack of chauvinism— and likely connected to it—that he'd remained immune to all the hype about great loveless sex had seemed a singular blessing (*see* Attitudes: Women; Biography/Summary; Love/Summary/General: Pleasure; and Sex/Considerations: Inhibition, lack of).

Satiety: Up until his last illness, the pair achieved satiety via daily lovemaking (with missed days often followed by a string of twice-daily sessions—though this was not a formula). Moreover, considering that once under the same roof they'd had full access to each other, and the regularity with which they actually made love, his unflagging urgency in regard to touching, smelling, tasting, and penetrating her had made her wonder where the urgency continued to come from, that is, whether he required an equal number of years of an intense sexuality to make up for his years of celibacy or, celibacy aside, he was just highly sexed, or both of the above (*see* Sex/Considerations: Celibacy, previous; Dependence, physical).

Taste: Repeatedly during their time together, she would try to recall when in past experience the way that she *tasted* had even been commented upon, never mind celebrated. Granted, previous partners had practiced cunnilingus but never with his ability or enthusiasm. Early on, he'd declared that his tongue was as sensitive as his penis, and it soon became obvious that in no way did he consider cunnilingus a mere component of foreplay or in any way secondary to intercourse so that (a) he spent almost as much time nibbling her pubic hair and licking her clitoris and/or vagina as he did being inside her and (b) his exclamations re her delicious taste and smell were evidence that the practice afforded him as much pleasure as herself. The single cloud on the horizon was her reluctance to return the compliment. Fellatio had never been her thing: It always made her jaws ache, and the fabulous taste he talked about either didn't exist in men or else, due to her lack of smell, didn't exist for her. Whatever, retreating into an "Ask him no questions, he'll tell you no lies" mode, she'd ultimately convinced herself that the pelvic manipulations she *did* like indulging in more than made up for its lack (*see* Sex: various; Sex/Involving: various; and Sex/Realities: Foreplay, Intercourse).

INVOLVING

Back: Stroking, kissing, and licking each other's back was an acknowledged, though not invariable, part of the couple's lovemaking. Of the two, he'd probably enjoyed it more, both as practitioner and recipient, since he hadn't shared her prejudices about the back *necessarily* being less sensitive than other parts of the body (*see* Sex/Involving: Breasts, Face).

Breasts: Traditionally, one of the outstanding sensations for her during sex was having her breasts—and particularly the nipples— mouthed. As she'd made a point of telling him as much right from the beginning, he'd been assiduous in the practice, though as it generally hadn't elicited either the cries of appreciation or moans that were always audible when he was occupied farther down, she'd had to assume that it afforded him less pleasure than cunnilingus. That said, now and then he had got sufficiently carried away as to be a bit painful (*see* Sex/Considerations: Odour, Taste).

Clitoris: *See* Sex/Considerations: Odour, Taste.

Ear: Re the two activities associated with the ear, the couple's preferences tended to vary. For her, nibbling the lobe had it all over sticking one's tongue inside, whereas for him the latter seemed to have been the more desirable. The reasons for this divergence are instructive. Her preference had stemmed from a chronic worry over how clean and/or wax-free he, she, or *anyone* could ever really get the inside of their ear, whereas his had been the result of a general predilection for all orifices or—though less likely given his lack of chauvinism—the simple fact that ear-tonguing was *supposed* to be a sexy thing to do (*see* Character: Chauvinism, lack of and Sex/ Considerations: Taste).

Face: Though not necessarily high on the list of physically sensitive areas, the face yet occupied a crucial niche in the couple's lovemaking because it happened to contain the only part of the anatomy—the eyes—where love could physically be expressed as well as made. And indeed, seeing each other look at, kiss, or otherwise touch every part of the other's face was held—by her absolutely and him to a certain degree—as among the most precious moments of any lovemaking session (*see* Sex/Realities: Kissing).

Fingers: For the duo, fingers had loomed significantly as objects of sensation. Chewing, sucking, or licking in between one finger and the next could generally be relied on to arouse either him or her and was often carried on with other activities in progress. In this regard, however, it must be said that his hands had been so unusually large, the jaw ache she otherwise associated with fellatio tended to be a risk if she continued too long at any finger activity bar licking (*see* Biography/Joint: Spectacles; Sex/Considerations: Taste; Sex/Involving: Palms).

Legs: Given that personally she'd always considered her legs ugly in the extreme, his absolute fascination with them during lovemaking had always been a sort of inexplicable dispensation, not unlike his delight with her odour and taste. That said, spirited sessions of his touching, licking, or kissing every part of them had not always been matched—leg for leg—with like attentions to his own limbs, even though (interestingly) the latter happened to have been extremely shapely and even objects of her envy (*See* Love/General: Monogamy and Sex/Considerations: Odour, Taste).

Mouth: During most lovemaking sessions—and aside from any sort of kissing—there was no part of the mouth of one that was not explored by the tongue of the other. While both enjoyed the activity, it cannot be denied that it required absolutely sweet breaths to be *thoroughly* enjoyable and occasionally—due, say to a particularly exotic meal or some other circumstance—the oral hygiene the pair always practiced before having sex would be insufficient for their guarantee. In such instances, the two would soon agree that the breaths of either one or both of them weren't up to it and the activity curtailed with no residual ill feelings (*see* Love/General: Openness and Sex/Realities: Kissing).

Palms: While she'd supposed that prior to him, mutual attention to the palms via kissing, licking, and/or nibbling had been a feature of sex with one or another partner, never before had she been made aware of the palms as quite so sensitive and endearing a part of the body. He, by comparison, was obviously a "palm-man" from way back, given both the amount of time he'd invariably lavished on hers and had expected to be lavished on his own in return (*see* Sex/Involving: Fingers).

Penis: *See* Sex/Considerations: Dependence, physical, Egyptian Dance, Menstruation, Taste and Sex/Involving: Vagina, various.

Pubic hair: During their time together, the couple had been pleased by and taken advantage of the pubic hair on offer—he via nibbling and she via face-rubbing. Indeed, *her* appreciation had extended to the aesthetic as unlike the hair on his head, his pubic hair had retained its original auburn colour. Her own, sad to say, had started going white even before they'd met, though neither this nor the fact that—either because of him or as a natural consequence of ageing—it had become significantly thinner than in her youth, had ever put him off (*see* Biography/His: Colouring, fair and Sex/Considerations: Taste).

Stomach: In referring to the stomach vis-à-vis the pair, a clear distinction must be maintained between the absolutely flat area between chest and groin with a navel in the middle belonging to him, and the depressingly curvy mound that increased just before menses and decreased—though never as much—thereafter (plus navel) belonging to her. The distinction is important as it tended to colour much of her attitude toward the area during lovemaking in that, navel notwithstanding, she'd had to remind herself that it *was* a stomach and not some undifferentiated part of his torso and thereby a special place for leaning one's cheek against while caressing with one's hands. He, by contrast, could never have doubted hers was anything else, and thus had remained free of all philosophical impediments regarding ministrations thereto (*see* Biography/His: Walk and Love/General: Monogamy).

Toes: *See* Sex/Involving: Fingers, Legs.

Vagina: While unquestionably it had rendered the acquisition of an effective diaphragm a tricky proposition over the years, the fact that her uterus was tilted to one side had unfailingly prompted comments from partners about how wonderful it felt inside her and their reluctance to ever have to emerge. Indeed, so inevitable were these comments that she'd tended to worry about an appropriate response. "That's great" was a definite mood killer, whereas "Thank you" made it sound as if she were trying to take undue credit. This last statement notwithstanding, though, it cannot be denied that knowledge of the abnormality and its consequence was a major factor when she'd told him on the phone she was "good" at sex, and that, given such hypocrisy, it had been both a relief and gratification when it became clear that he'd agreed with the general opinion (*see* Sex/Summary; Sex/Considerations: various; and Sex/Realities: Intercourse).

REALITIES

Ejaculation: One of the qualities he'd possessed as a lover was the ability to repeatedly bring himself just to the point of orgasm, then delay it and ejaculation and sort of start again. On occasion, he could dispense with ejaculation entirely and yet declare himself perfectly satisfied. When, at last, she couldn't resist telling him how impressed she was with such control, he'd replied that she needn't be—most mature men had it. To which *she'd* answered that on the contrary, never in all the years of her experience with mature men or men of any age had she come across anything like it, and, just once, it wouldn't kill him to take credit where credit was owing. Though he hadn't agreed, at the time the pair had been too knackered to discuss it further, and the subject had been dropped (*see* Character: Diffidence, Self-effacement; Sex/Considerations: Pleasure; and Sex/Realities: Orgasm).

Erections: Never, during their time together, had erections been difficult for him to come by, so to speak. Granted, they *had* varied in quality, but not even the once or twice that he'd tried a condom had they completely failed him, though the latter had happened to one or two other of her partners in the pre-him years. His very best erections were often independent of either of their efforts occurring, as they did, when he'd wake after a good night's sleep. Not surprisingly, morning came to be the favoured time for their lovemaking (*see* Biography/Hers: Quakers; Sex/Considerations: Birth control; and Sex/Realities/Intercourse).

Foreplay: *See* Sex/Considerations: Taste and Sex/Realities/Intercourse.

Intercourse: Prior to their relationship, she had had a very definite blueprint of what—technically speaking, anyway—constituted "successful" sex. It began with foreplay, then moved to intercourse, and finally reached mutual orgasm. If, for some reason, the three events did not occur in precisely that order or any of them was omitted, the encounter had failed. And then they'd begun a physical relationship and her blueprint went right out the window. For one thing, there seemed to be no mandatory order to what they did. What went by the name of foreplay (simply because it didn't include penetration) happened whenever—on occasion, even after orgasm—or else might be skipped altogether. The same could be said—though granted, very rarely—regarding intercourse itself, as he happened to be sufficiently skillful at cunnilingus to bring her to orgasm through it and satisfy himself in the process. In any case, for the time allowed them, some degree of the unexpected had generally characterized the couple's lovemaking sessions. Indeed, after his death more than once she'd wondered at what point a sexual routine would *have* emerged and of what it would have consisted (*see* Sex: all categories, various).

Kissing: During their time together, the couple considered kissing a vital part of lovemaking. As in other areas, preferences as to the style of kissing had varied with her ranking short kisses as more erotic than the long, drawn-out variety he happened to favour. Given that both were generally very alert to what pleased the other in bed, she'd soon concluded that he must dislike "her" style in the extreme since it never happened without a specific request and, even then, didn't go on for long. Untypically, she had decided not to ask why but instead had simply accommodated herself to what he *had* proffered (*see* Sex/Involving: Mouth).

Orgasm: *See* Sex/Considerations: Odour, Taste; Sex/Realities: Ejaculation, Intercourse.

Positions: Given that the sum of their respective ages had come to more than 100, the couple had been rather proud of the number of positions they were able to indulge in during lovemaking. The crowning achievement, in the opinion of both, had been the ability to come full circle, that is to move from him on top to her without his once having to withdraw. In fact, for a time both had been so chuffed about the manoeuvre that they couldn't resist doing it during every session. The latter situation had not lasted long, however. Very soon he'd warned her that their lovemaking was at risk of turning into a routine if they weren't more selective, and they'd become so immediately thereafter (*see* Sex/Realities: Intercourse).

T

Time

Summary
After his death, it was the consensus of opinion that although the couple had been granted precious little time together, such paucity was in fact ameliorated by the intensity of the relationship. That is, since (in an important sense) depth of feeling and experience thickened ordinary units of time, ergo, the couple's intense two years were equal to twenty of blander individuals. Actually, the arithmetic hadn't much impressed her. As balm for the soul, it sounded even less promising than the one about how eventually she would be glad they'd had any time at all. Of course, she couldn't deny that everything about the relationship *had* been acute: their courtship; her mother's death; their cohabitation and house experiences; and, throughout, their feelings for each other. Perhaps she might have come round to agreeing had most of the consolers not then observed that "time" was bound to heal the pain of her loss, and she'd wondered if *this* "time" was still the 10 to 1 variety. Because as far as she was concerned, her post-death feelings and experiences were, though diametrically opposite, yet every bit as powerful as those she'd had with him, and by that logic the same ratio ought to apply. And *that* meant she'd likely be dead before she ever got over his death. Ultimately, it had all been too confusing, and by the end of anybody's month or two, she'd more or less rejected the idea (*see* Biography: various; House: various; and Love: various).

Day: Day "times" for the couple were pretty much the same as for all lovers. Time moved unequally throughout each day, its pace dependent on whether they happened to be together (faster than a speeding bullet) or apart (slug speed). Granted, there could be—and often were—exceptions to both categories, such as absorption in one's work whisking the hours along or making love rendering them irrelevant. Generally speaking, however, the "together-apart" categories *had* applied—so much so that it was probably fortunate for the pair that they hadn't known how few days they were to have overall.

Future: *See* Love/Summary and Time: Past, Years.

Past: During their time together, the couple had come to understand that they were the possessors of "two pasts"—the first consisting of enormous lumps of pre-him and -her and the second of the small, shining nuggets they were jointly accumulating. While both lumps and nuggets had their function (the former, for example, being responsible for moulding the thinking, personality, and appearance of each and thereby the relationship), the nuggets were infinitely more precious because they reflected the happiest period of both their lives. The unique qualities of the latter were acknowledged by the two at the time and by her alone when the accumulation had ended and she had to face how few nuggets there were or ever could be. Indeed, after his death, she found it impossible to amalgamate the lumps and nuggets into one outlay so that like it or not, she was left with the same two pasts as previously and little interest as to a likely third (*see* Biography/His: various; Biography/Hers: various; Biography/Joint: various; and Time: Years).

Years: At least for as long as he was well, the couple were probably fonder of the year as a personal unit of time than of any other, barring days. This preference was rooted firstly in the conceit that the two masses of "pre" years—however uninspiring their contents compared to what they were experiencing together—had, as already mentioned, made them what they were and thus, by extension, created the relationship. Particularly important in this regard was the maturity that both felt had come with middle age. In another context, the year served as an important marker both for landmark celebrations, such as their first anniversary and, as it happened, her fiftieth birthday, as well as a pointer to a future which they'd tended to view in terms of twenty years, say, rather than two decades. Indeed, it was only after he was gone and all thoughts of a joint future brought to an abrupt end that she began to look upon every measurement of time (years included) as a sentence (*see* Biography/ Summary; Love/General: Anniversaries; Self-image/Contributing to: Age, Menopause; and Time: Past).

Transport

Summary

Prior to their time together, the couple's notions of covering distances beyond walking or cycling range had, as in numerous other ways, reflected their different backgrounds. He had grown up in an area inaccessible to public transport so that—first as a passenger and then as a driver—cars had always been a part of his life. She, by contrast, had spent her youth in a big city with all that implied re buses and subways; experienced, at the age of ten, the death of the sole driver in her family and the sale of the family car; and subsequently developed a medical condition that made it difficult for her to obtain a licence. So it was that only once, during the single other significant relationship in her life, that the concept of "her/driver" had actually surfaced on her mental horizon. Her other half in those days had suffered from a heart condition, and obviously worried by what might happen, she'd decided she ought to learn how to handle a car—at least to the extent of being able to go for help in an emergency. He'd agreed to teach her and duly found an unused airport for her lessons.

She hadn't really got the hang of it yet when his death—though neither at the wheel or even in the same city as herself—finished the instruction. Never one to miss out on cosmic significance, she'd seized upon both endings as a sign that henceforth she must remain dependent on others to ferry her about (*see* Biography: various; House/Summary/Miscellaneous: Appliances; and Illness/Chronic: Epilepsy).

Bicycle: Her image of him as an active, greeny sort of person had naturally included the ownership and use of bicycles. As it turned out, though he *had* owned several specimens, in their entire time together, she could only once recall him cycling, at the very beginning of their relationship, when he'd been late for his daughter's birthday dinner and his van had conked out and he'd had no choice. Other than that one time, his bicycle collection had tended to remain safely tucked away, unused. On the eve of their move to House No. 2, he had told her that once in the city, he *would* begin to cycle regularly but had done nothing of the sort. This failure had had to do with (a) having a house on top of a hill (though not as high a hill as they'd been perched on in the country); (b) the fact that where they lived did not go out of its way for cyclists, who often didn't have their own lane and (even more than pedestrians) were invariably choked by exhaust fumes from cars; and (c) the traditional laziness of the motorist. As to herself and bicycles, she'd cycled as a small child and right at the beginning of her stay in England, but then got out of the habit due to (d) fear of using *any* vehicle on the road because of her illness (as explained above); and (e) a streak of laziness probably surpassing his own, though of different vehicular causes (*see* Attitudes: Ecology, Population; Biography/Joint: Walks; Character: Laziness; Self-image/Contributing to: Exercise; and Transport: Car, Public).

Car: The couple owned two vehicles during their time together. The first was a minivan in which he'd hauled around his carpentry tools and such and into which, during her mother's visit to England, he'd installed a second set of seats—an impressive feat that had put his back out. The second was a Mini they'd christened Mini the Moocher. Chief memories of the Moocher included (a) the creation of and fitting her out with loose covers; (b) wondering how the hell he was ever going to get all those groceries into the car and seeing him do it every single time; (c) a steady stream of bills for her upkeep; (d) their embarrassment at her elderly aunt—during one of the only two European visits by members of her family during their relationship—finding it impossible to get into the backseat and having to walk back to their house from a neighbourhood restaurant; and (d) being able to park almost anywhere. Both times he had asked her if she didn't mind riding around in such modest transport and both times she'd answered that as long as the thing got from A to B, the rest didn't matter. *In fact,* she didn't believe people should own cars at all. That last statement, however, had been so much bravado. For as long as it lasted, it was damned lovely to have a set of wheels and the ability to pick up and go whenever and wherever one wanted (*see* Abilities: Sewing; Attitudes: Ecology; Biography/ Joint: Rituals; Illness/Chronic: Back pain; and Money/Summary: Bills).

Public: As stated above, public transport had been as fundamental to her as cars to him. Even when she'd begun to live in a place without an underground and the buses became privatised and their number increased to nuisance proportions, she remained deeply grateful for their existence. He, by contrast, had always appeared distinctly uncomfortable and out of place during the times she could recall him on a city bus. Whether he actually *felt* that way was something else again. She'd simply assumed as much due to his choice—nine times out of ten—of taking the Moocher into the city centre (with the attendant and increasingly frustrating searches for parking space that entailed) over using a bus. That said, his prejudice against public transport hadn't been universal.

For travelling distances between cities and such, he could be as content with a coach or train as a car, just as long as he didn't eat anything beforehand. Even her own use of public transport couldn't be said to have remained static, as after his death she began to walk into town because it helped to ease her heartache (*see* Biography/Hers: Epilogue; Illness/Chronic: Colitis, ulcerative; Self-image/Contributing to: Exercise; and Transport: Car).

$\mathcal{W}_{ills}$

Summary

If for no other reason than it presumed one's own death (and who wanted to think about *that*), she could not deny that drawing up a will wasn't a sobering exercise. Still, in the pre-him years it had been drummed into her head that regardless of one's age or physical condition, immediately one had property in any form it was vital to have a will, since possession of the latter saved a great deal of unseemly scrambling later on by one's survivors. Even had the proposition not *sounded* so sensible, personally witnessing just such behaviour—though scrambling hardly describes what was in reality close to a family war—over the modest possessions of a close friend who had died intestate had been quite sufficient to convince her. As regards the pair, the subject had first arisen at her behest after they'd sold their country house and her mother's estate had finally been settled. While initially he had reacted to her suggestion as if she were proposing unanesthetised root canal, after a week or so he'd got used to the idea, and (very fortunately given that in fact he would be dead by the following spring) they had proceeded (*see* House/Adventures: Sale; Money/Summary: Investment; and Wills: Attorney).

Attorneys: One of the things she could never get over during their time together was the number of attorneys she had in her employ. First there was the one she had in New York; then there was the one she had in England; and then there was *his* solicitor, whom she had just sort of adopted as her own as a partnerly act. That made three, although the pre-him man dropped out by default after a time. Perhaps it wasn't *just* the number of attorneys; perhaps it was also the investment counsellors and accountants on both sides of the ocean, the whole bunch compelling her to observe that slowly but surely, she was accumulating a larger staff than Rupert Murdoch (*see* Money/Summary: Investment).

Cremation: An inevitable part of drawing up any will involved deciding whether or not one wished to be buried or cremated. Without hesitation, both he and she had opted for cremation— though (a) why they did and (b) why they felt so strongly about it was somehow taken for granted by the pair rather than discussed. Perhaps the preference had to do with what had happened during their stay in New York. Her mother had died, been cremated, and (considering it ghoulish to keep them) she had decided to scatter her mother's ashes in the Hudson River—on a stretch of water parallel to the ten or so streets between the Metropolitan Opera House and a very exclusive shoe shop, called Botticelli's, these being her mother's two very favourite spots in the city. The scattering had required a ferry ride around Manhattan Island, though when they'd got to what she reckoned was the place, *he'd* been the one to do it; the wind had been in the wrong direction so that most of the ashes were blown onto him rather than settling where they should. After his own cremation, she wondered whether this hadn't been a bit of environmental augury. That said, the scattering of his own ashes on a very beautiful meadow near their country house had gone much more smoothly, even allowing for the several horses who'd then ambled up to eat the flowers that the mourners had strewn over them (*see* Biography/Joint: New York City).

Estates: Though the couple had insisted on identical wills, long after his was signed and sealed, hers was still generating exotic letters between English solicitor and American lawyer—a situation brought about (she assumed) by her and her money not residing in the same country. After a number of months, however, the English solicitor at last summoned the pair to his office and announced that he and his counterpart in New York were now in agreement over most of the will's provisions save the location of the trust fund for his share of her estate—a remark that precipitated the following exchange: **She:** "*What* trust fund? He's a big boy. He can have my money outright." **Solicitor:** "Really? But what if he then goes and marries someone you don't like?" **She:** "I'll be dead!" **Solicitor:** "Yes, but . . ." **She:** "If it really bothers me, I'll come back and haunt him." **Solicitor:** "Well, then—that makes things much easier." The meeting hadn't ended there, though. As it was plain from the couple's demeanour that they couldn't believe the solicitor had actually made such a comment, there then followed a lengthy recital by the latter of the situations he had met with in his professional experience, a monologue every bit as harrowing as anything ever uttered in Dickens or Balzac (*see* Money/Summary and Wills/Summary).

Inheritance: *See* Money/Summary and Wills/Summary.

*W*ork

Summary
Until he fell ill, the couple pursued their respective work more or less full time—she continuing a practise stretching back the length of her time in England, and he doing so for the first time in many years. As a playwright and visual artist, respectively, the pair's areas of interest had been sufficiently distinct to preclude competition so that throughout their time together wholesale encouragement of all new projects was the norm. Moreover, first attempts at collaboration between the two—in the form of (a) several sketches for a number of sets to a play she planned to write; (b) a fanciful series of portraits based on the protagonist of an already finished work; and (c) a chil-

dren's nonsense poem inspired by a series of illustrations he had done for another purpose—likewise characterised the period. While both were extremely grateful for the opportunity to be able to pursue their professions, due to a combination of factors including (a) a string of disappointments in the pre-him and -her years (though of the two, he had had *some* success); (b) lack of financial incentive; and (c) feelings of inferiority, which were second nature to him and which—at least in this area—she happened to share, recognition continued to elude them both. Their response to the above generally took the form of earnest conversations about (a) the uncanny similarity between promoting one's art and peddling underwear door-to-door and (b) how the former might be rendered less loathsome if only each would promote the other. Sadly, (b) never got past the idea stage, and the two had remained in their ivory tower. In fact, it was only when he was dying that her promise to "get him a reputation if it was the last thing she ever did" at last provided her with the drive and conviction she had lacked previously so that after his death she not only set about it with a vengeance but also wondered if at some point this newly discovered fortitude might not equally be applied to herself (*see* Art: all categories; Biography/His: Recession; Character: various; Money/Summary; Passions/Art: Wood; Self-image: various; and Work/Hers: Writing; Work/His: Book Illustration).

H E R S

Brissot, J. P.: Even on first acquaintance, Jacques-Pierre Brissot appeared to be a "character" in all the definitions of the word she demanded (i.e., a strong protagonist plus an extraordinary and endearing because fallible human being) and worthy of a place alongside all the other historical types she was addicted to writing plays about. In fact, so impressed was she with the eighteenth-century revolutionary that even the prospect of wading through untold books in French hadn't daunted her. On the contrary—any one man who could (a) do everything required of a would-be *philosophe,* all to no avail; (b) unfailingly get himself into debt via untenable and/or treasonable projects; (c) dabble with English Abolitionists to the point of finagling a trip to the United States; (d) return to Paris and be chucked into the Bastille, though briefly; (e) allegedly become a police spy; (f) subsequently throw himself body and soul into the French Revolution, thereby turning things around enough to resurface as (g) the prosperous editor of a revolutionary journal; (h) an elected representative of the municipality of Paris, the Legislative Assembly, and National Convention in that order; (i) virtual director of France's foreign policy in the early 1790s; (j) leader of a radical party destined to be undone by a more radical party; and (k) their guillotined victim—surely deserved her best efforts and a trek across the boards. As with so much else connected with Brissot, however, fate was to undo him yet again. This time his bad luck reached across a period of 200 years to nestle in the liver cancer of the lover of someone keen to write a play about him, thereby not merely preventing the latter from getting down to the play in question the whole time the lover was ill (even though she'd been just on the point of starting it) but rendering her emotionally incapable of doing so after the lover's death (*see* Illness/Last [His]: all categories; Passions/Miscellaneous: History; and Work/Hers: various).

Chartists: Occasionally before she'd honed in on an individual as subject, the *movement* the individual belonged to would have caught her eye. In this regard, the nineteenth-century Chartists were probably unique in that a number of circumstances (including those referred to above) prevented her from ever getting to the point of sorting out a single man or woman from its ranks. Not that those ranks with (a) a history of suffering and repression equal to that of any oppressed group in her own time; (b) their programme of change (in the form of a political charter); (c) the lack of consensus over how to achieve it, and (d) their defeat at the time (though ultimate victory)—weren't fascinating in their own right. It was simply that whenever she came to think of the Chartist movement, it was less as the breeding ground for the subject of some future play and more in terms of what they would have made out of the current, unceasing onslaught on the social legislation their struggle had helped to bring about (*see* Character: Morality and Work/Hers: Brissot, J. P.).

Kempe, M.: In the endearing because fallible stakes, there could be little doubt that the medieval English mystic, Margery Kempe, took the highest honours. Kempe was notorious for her uncontrollable holy weeping (church services and pilgrimages being her specialty) and the corollary that no amount of ejections by angry priests (from the former) and bands of pilgrims (from the latter) ever succeeded in curbing it. Still, one woman's foibles could be another's windfall: In her eyes, concentrating on the mystic's antisocial behaviour offered a writer the unusual opportunity of portraying two realities at once, namely, that of Kempe's contemporaries who saw her as hypocritical and attention-seeking and that of the woman herself who (constant prayers to stop the tears or at least limit them to when she was alone notwithstanding) seemed genuinely unable to express her religiosity more conventionally. Indeed, it was an opportunity that she hadn't been able to resist, and more than one stage play about the mystic had been the result—their number a testament to the author's chronic inability not to come down on one side or the other (*see* Passions/Miscellaneous: History and Work/Hers: Brissot, J. P., Writing).

Margarethe: Along with ill-fated revolutionaries and annoying representatives of God, the third historical type to gain her attention during their time together was "the succeeder against the odds." Enter one Margarethe, fourteenth-century queen of Denmark— a lady sufficiently endowed with ambition, foresight, shrewdness, and lack of moral considerations to unerringly make good on the opportunities destiny was forever chucking in her lap—as the following facts tend to demonstrate: (a) both her father, the king of Denmark, and the elected crown prince die shortly after her marriage to the king of Norway; (b) she has a son by the Norwegian king and nine years later her husband dies; (c) Norway being a hereditary kingdom, her son becomes king of the former and Denmark being an electoral one, he is *chosen* king of the latter; (e) as he is still a minor at the time, Margarethe becomes regent of both; (f) her son predeceases her; (g) she displaces her nephew, the king of Sweden, with her sister's grandson, who then nominally becomes king of Denmark, Norway, and Sweden, though in fact his great aunt rules all three kingdoms until her death. Her admiration for Margarethe is difficult to overstate. In an age overwhelmingly of male rulers, Margarethe was a power broker par excellence, managing not merely to lay hands on one kingdom but rope in two others as well—a political union that was to last into the following century. Her two plays about the Danish queen—one a long, consummately uneconomical screen-cum-teleplay with something over fifty characters (and concerning the latter's entire life and reign) not to mention a short stage play concentrating on Margarethe's relationship with the future patron saint of Sweden, Bridget, were indisputably her favourites (*see* Work/Hers: Brissot, J. P., Kempe, M., Screenplay).

Restoration: Her consideration of the Stuart Restoration as a source of possible play matter had probably been briefer than even her flirtation with the Chartists. For a start, it hadn't originated with her but as a response to a historian friend who, absolutely dotty about King Charles II, had been getting encouraging noises from some of his pals in television and wondered if she'd be interested in collaborating on what sounded like (if she'd correctly understood) a walking-talking apologia for the Merry Monarch—replete with gorgeous costumes. She'd politely answered that (a) apologias really weren't her thing; (b) surely other Restoration figures whose personalities were a bit more—well—circumspect would provide better dramatic subjects because (c) even *he* couldn't deny that Charles II was so *obvious*—immediately adding that (d) she'd gladly look into the identities of such individuals if he wished. The historian being beyond speech at this point, she'd taken his silence for assent. In the event, several weeks later she learned that the friend was dropping the project because the telly interest had evaporated—and that had been that for her as well (*see* Work/Hers: Chartists).

Screenplay: The term *screenplay* and its poor sister, *teleplay,* were, in her mind, ultimately moveable, if not interchangeable, feasts principally due to a combination of (a) a sort of metaphysical speculation that there couldn't really be *that* much difference between them and (b) the mindset that results from forever writing things on spec. So it was that she was always prepared to rework any and all of her "screenplays" into "teleplays" or vice versa if the occasion should ever warrant. In any case, whether for the big screen or small, because *he* had made films, during their time together she became increasingly aware of the camera's function and at times had positively littered this scene or that with such terms as *long shot, crosscutting, tracking shot, close-up,* and *fade-out* (*see* Passions/Cinema: Cinema; Work/Hers: Margarethe, Writing; and Work/His: Film).

Writing: Ever since childhood, she had wanted to be a writer and duly scribbled away at one thing or another. Interestingly (given her output during their time together) her first attempts at age seven had also involved writing plays. These were five-page one-act comedies expressly written for and sent to a maternal great uncle whose residence near Hollywood was in her mind prima facie evidence of a connection with the movies—a belief she refused to abandon even after her parents had explained that Great Uncle X was in ladies' sportswear. Other memories from that time include (a) teaching herself how to type and taking over the family Underwood;

(b) occasionally being so convulsed with laughter at her own humour as to collapse over its keyboard; (c) being told by her parents that her plays were *trite*—a word she'd had to look up in the dictionary; and (d) not knowing *what* her great uncle thought of them, since she never put her name to what she wrote—this circumstance having less to do with her parents' opinion than the fact that Great Uncle X was the proverbial rich uncle in the family and she didn't want him to think she was after his money. After that, there seems to be a hiatus in peculiarly "writing memories" until her late twenties, when she'd turned to poetry. True, in the interim period she *had* come to realise that (e) she'd never attempt a novel because they were chock-full of descriptive passages that she always skipped over and would, therefore, hardly wish to write and (f) Mother (her father was already dead) wasn't ever likely to encourage her efforts due to—well-founded, as it happened—fears of this writing lark interfering with her daughter's *true* function on the planet, namely, becoming an elementary school teacher and getting married. Her involvement with poetry had perhaps been somewhat unusual in that it had been born of an intoxication with the *sound* of words and a desire to create verbal music rather than a burning need to say something. In that regard, she had actually studied musical composition for a brief time to sharpen her ear. Looking back over the poetry years, she would have to say that a growing proficiency in the form was in the end out-finessed by raw bad luck as in (a) thinking her reputation made when a quite famous poet raved over her work only to then find the latter not merely forgetting about it but her as well soon thereafter; (b) reading a rejection letter that listed her only fault as having chosen a subject the editor felt *she* knew more of (and presumably should write about); and (c) having another clutch of poems provisionally accepted by a publisher and then rejected because their advocate suddenly resigned. This final blow had, in the immediate pre-him years, pushed her in the direction of historical plays—the latter having the dual advantage of being mostly dialogue while at the same time catering to her passion for history. Thus had Playwriting Mark II proceeded until his death, when the whole question of writing—both in terms of what she'd already done and what she might embark on next—was thrown into limbo (*see* Abilities: Computer, Letter writing; Beliefs: Immortality; Character: Heroism; Love/General: Sentimentality; Music/Summary; Passions/ Miscellaneous: History; and Work/Summary/Hers: various).

HIS

Animation: Of all the special effects she had come across in his early films, none had intrigued her more than his experiments with animation. Somewhat surprisingly—as he was an artist and could have *drawn* whatever characters he wanted—he'd opted instead for the three-dimensional variety and had fashioned small, deliberately crude clay figures that had moved around with very simple gestures. Still, he hadn't actually been *adverse* to drawn cartoon figures. Though, as far as she was aware, he had never got as far with it as the clay figures, she also seemed to recall a storyboard for a very bizarre cartoon involving altered perceptions of reality in the most disturbing colours he could put together—overall, very much à la his more angst-filled paintings, and definitely nothing to amuse the kiddies with before they went to bed (*see* Art/Summary/Styles: Experimental and Passions/Cinema: Cinema).

Art: *See* Art: all categories and Biography/His: Recession.

Book illustration: Both in the pre-her years and to some extent during their time together, he had been involved in illustrating children's books—none (sadly) ever making it into print even though he had usually been paid by the authors. The first time he'd shown her a cross-section of the illustrations—and quite allowing for the love factor in her judgment—she'd been immensely impressed. They were (a) both literally and conceptually colourful;

(b) every bit as accomplished as any drawings in his usual style (which, after all, they were another form of); and (c) utterly charming. What she *hadn't* been able to judge, however, was the quality of the stories they accompanied—children (let alone their reading matter) not being a particular area of interest. Such deficiency, however, hadn't prevented her from being inspired to write a "children's poem" based on one of the only series of his illustrations to be rejected by the individual who'd commissioned them. The drawing in question had been intended for the cover and showed a big white bear lounging in a deck chair: one leg crossed over the other; arms behind head and wearing a man's hat and sunglasses. To her, the bear had seemed grooviness incarnate; visions of an up-market, "Paddington-Bear-for-the-Nineties" had swum before her eyes; she'd immediately dubbed the creation "O'Hare (*The* Bear)" and in less than a day written a twelve-verse nonsense epic about O'Hare's adventures. Though he'd been sufficiently tickled by the poem to subsequently create an accompanying storyboard, the appropriate agent hadn't, and poem and storyboard were turned down the single time the pair tried to place it—thereby illustrating (as it were) that however gifted and/or experienced the artist, nonmaternals like herself had no business being inspired *by anything* to write for children (*see* Art/Concepts: Imagination; Art/Forms: Drawing; Art/Materials: Coloured pencils; Attitudes; and Children).

Carpentry: Though both largely pre-dated their time together, she was nonetheless extremely sensible of the connection between the pieces he'd turned out as a carpenter and the work he'd produced as a sculptor. Indeed, the two were probably more points on a continuum than connected entities—as she'd discovered from her very first browse through the catalogue he'd put together for his carpentry business. Designed to entice future customers, what had enticed *her* was the unfailing presence of the twists and curves so familiar from his sculpture whenever he'd been allowed the slightest leeway in the design of the kitchen cabinet or garden trellis or sofa frame. Though he wouldn't have necessarily agreed—having pursued sculpture and carpentry independently—as far as wood was concerned, he'd been the complete artisan, that is, a throwback to a mythic Golden Age when "Art" and "Craft" hadn't been antithetical, and a natural mix of practicality and beauty were expected from the same object (*see* Abilities: Do-It-Yourself; Art: various; Attitudes: Ecology; Character: Heroism; House: various; and Work/His: Joinery).

Documentary: *See* Passions/Cinema: Cinema.

Eclecticism: Unfortunately, at least insofar as establishing a reputation, he had been as eclectic in his choice of art *forms* as in what he'd chosen to represent in whatever form he'd light upon. A possible career as a filmmaker, for example (and if the one documentary she'd seen was anything to judge by) seemed to have been done in more by *his* version of the bad luck that had plagued her as a poet than by particular weaknesses in the actual work. Ditto for his book illustrations, though at least in that instance, he'd generally been paid. Perhaps the real problem was being talented in just too many areas—the late twentieth century having as little use for a Renaissance man as an artisan (*see* Art/Concepts: Imagination; Passions/Cinema: Cinema; Work/Hers: Writing; and Work/His: Book illustration).

Joinery: Once, during one of the periodic outdoor fetes they used to throw while living in the country, a friend had commented on how glorious their garden looked. As its creator was temporarily in the house on some errand, she'd felt able to launch into a lengthy gush not only on his gardening, but on the vast range of his talents (speaking quickly, however, in case he suddenly came back). The monologue had brought smiling nods from the friend (who'd known him longer than herself)—at least until she'd mentioned "carpentry" when not a little offended, the friend had protested: "He's *not* a carpenter! Any idiot that knocks a nail into a piece of wood is a carpenter. He's a joiner—a cabinet maker." It had been an interesting distinction to hear about, since there was no question that *he* had always thought of and referred to himself as the former. Some days later, she had looked up both "carpentry" and "joinery" in the dictionary. The friend had been right. Carpentry involved woodwork of the solid bulk variety (such as buildings or ships), whereas joinery meant the production of lighter, more delicate objects, such as house fittings and furniture. That said, given that (a) the dictionary hadn't mentioned either being a nobler calling than the other, and (b) he no longer happened to be involved in *any* sort of woodwork as a livelihood, she had deemed it prudent to keep the nicety to herself (*see* Abilities: various; Love/General: Openness; and Work/His: Carpentry).

INDEX